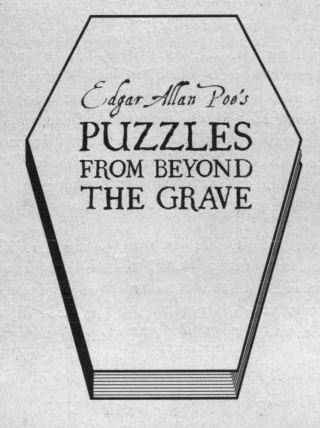

Edgar Allan Poe's
PUZZLES
FROM BEYOND
THE GRAVE

THIS IS A CARLTON BOOK

Published by Carlton Books Ltd
20 Mortimer Street
London W1T 3JW

Copyright © 2018 Carlton Books Ltd

A CIP catalogue for this book is available from the British Library.

ISBN 978-1-78739-102-4
Editorial: Chris Mitchell
Text and puzzles: Jason Ward
Design: Andri Johannsson
Picture research: Steve Behan
Puzzle checker: Neil Pyatt and Rich Galland
Production: Yael Steinitz

Printed in Dubai

The publishers would like to thank the following sources for
their kind permission to reproduce the pictures in this book.

Alamy: 19th era: 150; /AF Fotografie: 189; /Age Fotostock: 52; /The Artchives: 88, 102-103; /Artokoloro Quint Lox Limited: 125, 181; / Classic Image: 96-97, 149; /Granger Historical Picture Archive: 17, 106-107, 178-179; /Historical Images Archive: 154; /Interfoto: 65; /DeAgostini: 140-141; /Lebrecht Music and Arts Photo Library: 109, 129; /Oldtime: 80; /Past Art: 168; /The Print Collector: 110-111; /Universal History Archive/UIG : 86-87; /Walker Art Library: 164-165; /World History Archive: 83

Bridgeman Images: 30-31; /Bibliotheque Nationale, Paris, France: 21; /© British Library Board. All Rights Reserved: 10-11, 58; /Peter Jackson Collection: 24

Getty Images: 32, 42, 94, 100-101, 136-137, 138-139, 171, 175; /Culture Club: 60, 68; /Hulton Archive: 9, 77; /The Print Collector: 118-119

Mary Evans Picture Library: 74-75, 116, 133, 135, 158-159, 161, 187

Public Domain: 14-15, 18, 26, 85, 115, 198-199

Rex: British Library/Robana/REX/Shutterstock: 35

Shutterstock.com: AMN: 54-55; /Alexander P: 144; /Alvor: 156; /Amzhylttay: 143; /Alex74: 121; /Babich Alexander: 48, 49, 50, 76; /Berdsigns: 38-39, 46; /Bioraven: 13; /Bogadeva1983: 51; /Crystal Eye Studio: 183; /Danussa: 167; /Epine: 108, 123; /Fresher: 12-13; /Grop: 41; /Jivopira: 47; /Jumpingsack: 56-57; / Ksana-art: 4, 20; /Kseniakrop: 196-197; /Maria Kuza: 194-195; /Lablochki: 22; /La Puma: 90; /MaKars: 8, 66-67, 163; /Macrovector: 63; /Marzolino: 130-131, 145, 146; /Marzufello: 45; Elizaveta Melentyeva: 122; /MoreVector: 92-93, 98-99; /Moriz: 151; /Morphart Creation: 29, 36-37, 104-105, 152, 153, 185, 193; / Hein Nouwens: 7, 78-79, 112; /Onkachura: 12 (top); /Elena Paletskaya: 166; /Perunika: 172, 176-177; /Sketch Master: 188; /Time Trip: 200; /Bodor Tivadar: 130, 184, 191; /Vectorgoods Studio: 91; /Yoko Design: 70-71

Topfoto.co.uk: Granger Collection: 72-73

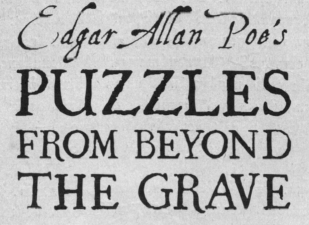

Edgar Allan Poe's
PUZZLES
FROM BEYOND
THE GRAVE

Cryptic Conundrums from the World
and Works of the Gothic Genius

CARLTON
BOOKS

JASON WARD

Contents

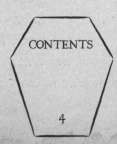

CONTENTS

4

Contents

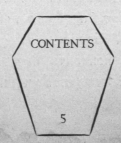

CONTENTS

Contents

CONTENTS

6

Contents

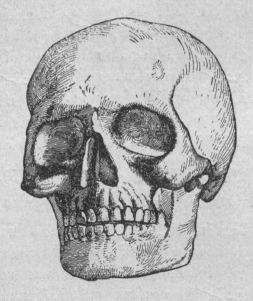

CONTENTS

7

Introduction:
The Case of the Hidden Case

Blame Rufus Wilmot Griswold. In a final ill-advised decision after a lifetime of ill-advised decisions, Edgar Allan Poe named his general nemesis and one-time love rival as his literary executor. Given his temperament, it would have been difficult for Poe to name someone who wasn't an enemy to some degree or another, but he could have chosen no-one worse.

Two days after Poe's death, Griswold wrote a blistering obituary stating, "this announcement will startle many, but few will be grieved by it" and went on to qualify Poe as "little better than a carping grammarian", then spent the remaining eight years of his life seeking to obliterate Poe's reputation.

The public's perception of Poe as an addled, tormented madman calcified during these years, and nearly two centuries later we're still trying to figure out who exactly—beyond one of the greatest, strangest, darkest, most influential writers of his era—was Edgar Allan Poe.

That the question has never been satisfactorily answered may be due in some part to the fittingly peculiar manner of his demise: Poe disappeared from his Baltimore home in late September 1849 and was found a week later, delirious in a tavern in someone else's shoddy clothes. He died in hospital a few days later, repeatedly calling out the name "Reynolds" for reasons that no-one has ever been able to ascertain. The author's missing week and the circumstances of his death are one of the great unsolved mysteries in the history of literature, prompting theories from cholera to a brain tumour to Poe being forcibly intoxicated by a "cooping gang" in order to vote multiple times in a sheriff's election.

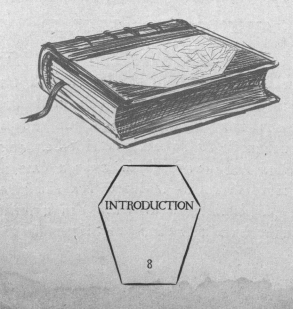

Such unknowability has long fed intense speculation about a writer whose work already inspired intense speculation. There was cause for some excitement, then, when the *Baltimore Sun* reported last spring that a trunk discovered in an attic in Fordham, New York, was found to contain heavily corrected manuscripts in Poe's handwriting. At first it was thought that these were selected early drafts of his short stories and poems, but closer inspection by researchers at the Division of Rare and Manuscript Collections at Cornell University has produced a truly astonishing revelation: for each of his major works, from *The Raven* to *The Tell-Tale Heart* to *The Fall of the House of Usher*, Poe wrote and hid *secret* alternate versions that diverged from the original texts in order to pose fiendish conundrums, enigmas, maths puzzles and logic problems.

Poe—like many degenerate show-offs—loved puzzles, once boasting, "Nothing intelligible can be written which, with time, I cannot decipher", but why he chose to covertly lace his stories with them is as big a mystery as what he was up to between 27th September and 3rd October 1849.

Nevertheless, we present to you—for the first time ever—the secret works of Edgar Allan Poe.

THE MASQUE OF THE RED DEATH

A Thief In The Night

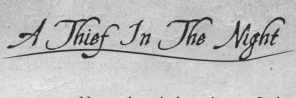

No pestilence had ever been so fatal, or so hideous.
Blood was its avatar and its seal—the redness and the horror
of blood. There were sharp pains, and sudden dizziness,
and then profuse bleeding at the pores, with dissolution.
But Prince Prospero was happy and dauntless and sagacious.
When his dominions were half depopulated, he summoned
to his presence a thousand hale and light-hearted friends
from among the knights and dames of his court, and with
these retired to the deep seclusion of one of his castellated
abbeys. The courtiers, having entered, brought furnaces and
massy hammers and welded the bolts.

With such precautions they might bid defiance to
contagion, and the prince had provided all the appliances
of pleasure. There were buffoons, there were improvisatori,
there were harlequins, there were ballet dancers, there were
musicians, there was Beauty, there was wine. There were
also two knights who woke up on the second morning,
weak-kneed and gaunt.

THE
MASQUE
OF THE RED
DEATH

12

Prince Prospero hastened to the knights' quarters, his usual gaiety dislodged by **fury**. He asked them if they'd encountered anyone with scarlet stains on their body before entering the abbey, and they both replied that no, they had just revelled too freely in the spirit of the previous evening. The first knight, suppressing a shiver, begged: "My Duke, do you not believe us? Either I am a liar or my compatriot is telling the truth!"

Had the knights contracted the Red Death?

THE MASQUE OF THE RED DEATH

13

Solution on page 202

THE
MASQUE
OF THE RED
DEATH

14

Solution on page 202

Landlocked Landed Gentry

Of those thousand hale and light-hearted friends summoned by the Prince, 810 held titles—knights, dames, marquesses, countesses, vassals, viscounts and viceroys. Improbably, there was even a couple of edelherrs, skartabels and a baronet who'd appeared from parts unknown. If it hadn't been evident before, it became demonstrable that nobility lasts longer than wealth: 630 of the revellers had fortunes, while a hundred had neither a title nor a fortune to their name.

How many of the abbey's new inhabitants had both a fortune and a title?

Prince Prospero's abbey was the only stronghold against the bane that stalked his lands. It was an extensive and magnificent structure, the creation of his own eccentric yet august taste. A strong and lofty wall girdled it in. This wall had gates of iron. Before the courtiers entered and welded the bolts behind them, they stood guard as the prince's friends arrived in a procession of stagecoaches, untroubled laughter seeping out from the back seats. To enter the abbey, each guest was required to answer a riddle, the solution of which—fortunately for them—they had already been gifted. The question was:

What is it that every living person has seen, but will never see again?

THE
MASQUE
OF THE RED
DEATH

THE
MASQUE
OF THE RED
DEATH

17

Solution on page 202

The "Red Death" had long devastated the country, but the external world could take care of itself. In the meantime it was folly to grieve, or to think. Toward the close of the fifth or sixth month of his seclusion, and while the **pestilence** raged most furiously abroad, Prince Prospero entertained his friends at a masked ball of the most unusual magnificence.

It was a voluptuous scene, that masquerade. But first let me tell of the rooms in which it was held. There were five—an imperial suite. Each room's windows were of stained glass whose colour varied in accordance with the prevailing hue of the decorations of the chamber into which it opened. The chamber at the eastern extremity was hung, for example, in blue—and vividly blue were its windows. The second chamber was purple in its ornaments and tapestries, and here the panes were purple. The third was green throughout, and so were the casements, while the fourth was furnished and lit with orange. The fifth apartment was closely shrouded in black velvet tapestries that hung all over the ceiling and down the walls, falling in heavy folds upon a carpet of the same material and hue. But in this chamber only, the colour of the windows failed to correspond with the decorations. The panes here were scarlet—a deep blood red.

Prior to the ball, four married couples had been staying in the different apartments, all wisely eschewing the final one. There were several facts about this arrangement that one could consider. For instance, Venerio was not staying in the purple chamber, Galitia was not married to Antonio, and Girardino was residing in the orange apartment. Also, Maso was not married to Corelia, Caterina was one of the wives and Venerio had not been living in the green chamber while Galitia very much had. Finally, Corelia was married to Venerio and Maria was not married to Girardino.

Which couples were staying in which chambers?

THE
MASQUE
OF THE RED
DEATH

19

Solution on page 202

In the black chamber the effect of the firelight that streamed upon the dark hangings through the blood-tinted panes was ghastly in the extreme, and produced so wild a look upon the countenances of those who entered that there were few of the company bold enough to set foot within its precincts at all.

It was notable that the courtiers had resolved to leave means of neither ingress or egress, wary of the sudden impulses of despair, or even frenzy, from within. The Prince's boarders largely avoided the temptation of morbid thought, but upon entering that dark chamber they couldn't help outbursts of violent recrimination. The most concerning instance occurred when two of the guests, Scarlatto and Luzio, fought a duel of honour with daggers drawn. Each stabbed their opponent through the heart, yet neither died.

How did Scarlatto and Luzio survive?

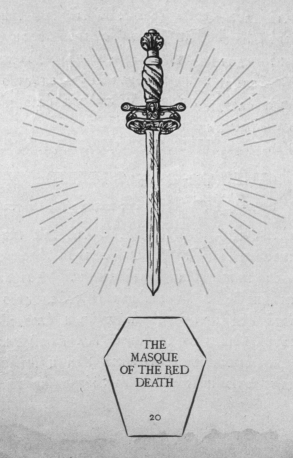

THE
MASQUE
OF THE RED
DEATH

THE
MASQUE
OF THE RED
DEATH

21

Solution on page 202

THE
MASQUE
OF THE RED
DEATH

22

The masquerade held much of the beautiful, much of the wanton, much of the bizarre, something of the terrible, and not a little of that which might have excited disgust. But not yet: it takes time for libations to loosen the noumenon.

At the beginning of the grand fête there were only four knights and four dames with the courage to involve themselves in the festivities. Each dance called for mixed couples, so a knight and a dame would dance opposing another knight and dame. No person danced alongside or opposing another person more than once, and yet over three successive dances they all danced together in two rooms.

How did they accomplish this?

THE
MASQUE
OF THE RED
DEATH

23

Solution on page 203

THE
MASQUE
OF THE RED
DEATH

24

For those within the Prince's dominions but without the fortune of a good background, the only chance for sanctuary was to have a talent in court entertainment. A family of performing brothers was specifically recruited for this task: Amadore, Agnolo, Andreuccio, Atenulf and Aiulf, who were a buffoon, an improvisatore, a ballet dancer, a musician and a harlequin.

The brothers always performed in the same order, and the night of the Prince's masquerade was no exception. The buffoon came on after Amadore and Atenulf but before the musician. The ballet-dancer came on third. Neither the harlequin nor Andreuccio was the first or last to perform. Agnolo, Amadore and Atenulf performed in that order.

What was each brother's act and in which order did they perform?

THE
MASQUE
OF THE RED
DEATH

25

Solution on page 203

Before the last echoes of the last chime had sunk into silence, there were many in the crowd who had become aware of a masked figure which had arrested the attention of no single individual before. The figure was tall and gaunt, and shrouded from head to foot in the habiliments of the grave. The mask which concealed the visage was made so nearly to resemble the countenance of a stiffened corpse that the closest scrutiny would have had difficulty in detecting the cheat. The mummer had gone so far as to assume the type of the Red Death. His vesture was dabbled in blood— and his broad brow, in common with all the features of the face, was besprinkled with the scarlet **horror**. He pointed a finger at Prince Prospero, and spoke:

"What does man love more than life,
Fear more than death or mortal strife,
What the poor have, the rich require,
And what contented men desire,
What the miser spends and the spendthrift saves
And all men carry to their graves?"

The Prince, maddening with rage, rushed through the chambers, while none followed on account of a deadly terror that had seized upon all. He bore aloft a dagger, and approached to within three or four feet of the retreating figure, when the latter turned suddenly and confronted his pursuer. There was a sharp cry— and the **dagger** dropped gleaming upon the sable carpet, upon which, instantly afterwards, fell prostrate in death the very same Prince Prospero.

And now was acknowledged the presence of the Red Death. And one by one dropped the revellers in the blood-bedewed halls of their revel, and each did die in the despairing posture of his fall. And the life of the ebony clock went out with that of the last of the gay. And the flames of the tripods expired. And Darkness and Decay and the Red Death held illimitable dominion over all.

What is the answer to the riddle posed by the Red Death?

THE
MASQUE
OF THE RED
DEATH

27

Solution on page 203

Three Eloquent Words

Only a couple of Edgar Allan Poe's works were explicitly designed as riddles; in this poem, he hid the name of its recipient in its lines.

For her this rhyme is penned, whose luminous eyes,
Brightly expressive as the twins of Lœda,
Shall find her own sweet name, that, nestling lies
Upon the page, enwrapped from every reader.
Search narrowly the lines!—they hold a treasure
Divine—a talisman—an amulet
That must be worn **at heart**. Search well the measure—
The words—the syllables! Do not forget
The trivialest point, or you may lose your labor!
And yet there is in this no Gordian knot
Which one might not undo without a sabre,
If one could merely comprehend the plot.
Enwritten upon the leaf where now are peering
Eyes scintillating soul, there lie **perdus**
Three eloquent words oft uttered in the hearing
Of poets, by poets—as the name is a poet's, too.
Its letters, although naturally lying
Like the knight Pinto—Mendez Ferdinando—
Still form a synonym for Truth.—Cease trying!
You will not read the riddle, though you do the best you **can do**.

Who was he writing it for?

A
VALENTINE

A
VALENTINE

29

Solution on page 204

The Conqueror Worm

It may be asserted that no event is so well adapted to inspire the
supremeness of bodily and mental distress as burial before death.
The unendurable oppression of the lungs—the stifling fumes of the damp
earth—the clinging to the death garments—the rigid embrace of the
narrow house—the **blackness** of the absolute Night—the silence like a sea
that overwhelms—these considerations carry into the heart a degree of
appalling and intolerable horror from which the most daring imagination
must recoil.

We know that there are diseases in which occur total cessations of
all the apparent functions of vitality, and yet these are merely
suspensions, pauses in the incomprehensible mechanism.
A certain period elapses and some unseen mysterious
principle again sets in motion the magic pinions and the
wizard wheels. Apart from the inevitable conclusion
that such cases must naturally give rise, now and then,
to premature interments, we have direct testimony to
prove that a vast number have actually taken place.
And thus what I have now to tell is of my
own actual experience.

For several years I had been subject to attacks of the singular disorder which physicians have agreed to term catalepsy. Although its causes are still mysterious, the disease's obvious and apparent character is well understood. Sometimes the patient lies, for a day only, or even for a shorter period, in a species of exaggerated lethargy. He is senseless and externally motionless; but the pulsation of the heart is still faintly perceptible; some traces of warmth remain; a slight colour lingers within the centre of the cheek; and, upon application of a mirror to the lips, we can detect a torpid, unequal, and vacillating action of the lungs. Sometimes the trance lasts for weeks—even for months; while the most rigorous medical tests, fail to establish any distinction between the state of the sufferer and what we conceive of absolute death.

The true curse of this malady is that the sufferer is aware of everything that is happening to them, with only the occasional lapses into insensibility sparked by the anguish of the predicament: during one such attack, as I suffered so, I became aware of a language entirely foreign to me. I somehow knew that "Maj hirmak spek" meant "Appearing trapped not", "Ruv spek twel" meant "Help trapped man", and "Lursy maj ruv" meant "Dead appearing man." As the hours slipped by in a dull lethargic consciousness of life and those who surrounded my bed, I tore my mind into pieces trying to answer the question:

How could I say "HELP NOT DEAD" in this strange tongue?

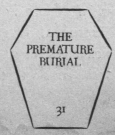

THE
PREMATURE
BURIAL

31

Solution on page 205

THE
PREMATURE
BURIAL

32

My nerves became thoroughly unstrung, and I fell prey to perpetual horror. I hesitated to indulge in any exercise that would carry me from home. In fact, I no longer dared trust myself out of the immediate presence of those who were aware of my proneness to catalepsy, lest, falling into one of my usual fits, I should be buried before my real condition could be ascertained.

I entered into a series of elaborate precautions, remodelling my family **vault** so it could be readily opened from within. The slightest pressure upon a long level would case the iron portals to fly back.

There were arrangements also for the free admission of air and light, and convenient receptacles for food and water, within immediate reach of the coffin intended for my reception. This coffin was warmly and softly padded, and provided with a lid, fashioned upon the principle of the vault-door, with the addition of springs so contrived that the feeblest movement would set it at liberty.

Besides all this, there was suspended from the roof of the tomb, a large bell, the rope of which, it was designed, should extend through a hole in the coffin, and so be fastened to one of the hands of the corpse. But, alas! what avails the vigilance against the Destiny of man? Not even these well-contrived securities sufficed to save from the uttermost agonies of living inhumation, a **wretch** to these agonies foredoomed!

I consulted with the region's finest physicians and scholars of bodily science. One told me that the odds of a grave outcome were "merely" 10 percent of 90 percent of 80 percent, considering the precautions I had taken, but I couldn't deduce what my chances of being prematurely interned were, and even if that were possible, my mortal terrors would listen to no reason—would accept no consolation.

What were my chances of being prematurely interned?

THE
PREMATURE
BURIAL

33

Solution on page 206

At length the slight quivering of an eyelid; I found myself emerging from total unconsciousness into the first feeble and indefinite sense of existence. Immediately thereupon, an electric shock of a **terror**, deadly and indefinite, sending the blood in torrents from the temples to the heart. I feel that I am not awaking from ordinary sleep. I recollect that I have been subject to catalepsy. And now, at last, as if by the rush of an ocean, my shuddering spirit is overwhelmed by the one grim Danger.

I endeavour to shriek; and my lips and my parched tongue move convulsively together in the attempt—but no voice issues from the cavernous lungs, which, oppressed as if by the weight of some incumbent mountain, gasp and palpitate. I feel that I lay upon some hard substance; and by something similar my sides are also closely compressed. I violently throw up my arms, which had been lying at length, with the wrists crossed. They strike a solid wooden substance, which extended above my person at an elevation of not more than six inches from my face. I can no longer doubt that I reposed within a coffin at last.

And now, amid all my infinite miseries, came sweetly the cherub Hope—for I thought of my precautions. I writhe, and make spasmodic exertions to force open the lid: it would not move. I feel my wrists for the bell-rope: it is not to be found. Despair reigns triumphant; for I can not help perceiving the absence of the paddings which I had so carefully prepared. The conclusion was irresistible. I was **not** within the vault.

Confronted with my fate, my mind vaults into madness of a manner I had never experienced before. In my stark, uncomprehending terror I am consumed by the notion that there are 10 throps in a slem, 6 slems in a gror, 5 grors in a wah, and 7 wahs in a pleem. What this meant I could not understand, yet the jagged edges of it sit in my brain. There comes to my nostrils the strong **peculiar** odour of moist earth, yet all I can think about is—

What is the number of throps in a pleem divided by the number of slems in a wah?

THE
PREMATURE
BURIAL

34

Solution on page 206

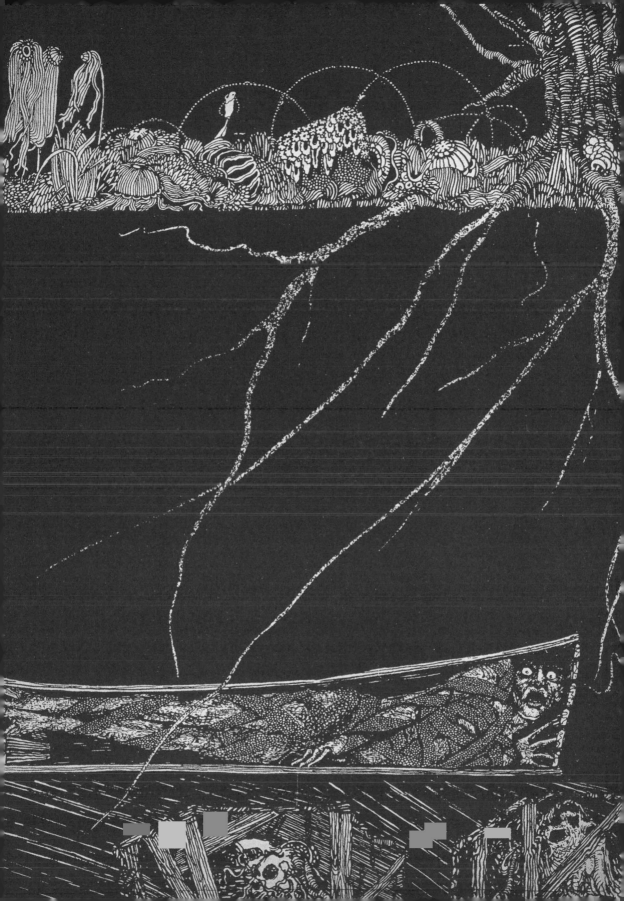

Demons On The Oxus

It was evident that I had fallen into a trance while absent from home—
while among strangers—when, or how, I could not remember—and it was
they who had buried me as a dog—nailed up in some common coffin—and
thrust, deep, deep, and for ever, into some ordinary and nameless **grave**.
As this awful conviction forced itself, thus, into the innermost chambers
of my soul, I once again struggled to cry aloud. And in this second
endeavour I succeeded. A long, wild, and continuous shriek, or yell, of
agony resounded through the realms of the subterranean Night.
"What the devil's the matter now!" said a gruff voice, in reply.

"Get out o'that! What do you mean by yowling in that 'ere kind of
style, like a cattymount?" said a second; and hereupon I was seized and
shaken without ceremony for several minutes by a junto of rough-looking
individuals. They did not arouse me from my slumber—for I was wide-
awake when I screamed—but they restored me to the full possession
of my memory.

Accompanied by a friend, I had proceeded, some miles down the banks of the James River. Night approached, and we were overtaken by a storm. The cabin of a small sloop lying at anchor in the stream, and laden with garden mould, afforded us the only available shelter. We made the best of it, and passed the night on board. The berth which I occupied had no bedding of any kind, and I found it a matter of exceeding difficulty to squeeze myself in. The whole of my vision arose naturally from the circumstances of my position and from my ordinary bias of thought.

The **tortures** I endured were inconceivably hideous, but out of Evil proceeded Good. My soul acquired temper. I went abroad. I discarded my medical books. No more bugaboo tales—**such as this**. In short I became a new man, and lived a man's life. I thought upon other subjects than Death; even on that first, new morning of my life, there was mystery and peculiarity to behold.

Those first two individuals—rough-looking though they were, told me of their lives and loves—of how they had fallen in love with each other's mothers, and how their sons now played together along the banks of the river. Once I would have nodded absently, but now I listened. I was even free to assist them when one of them pondered what relationship their two children had to one another. From that memorable night, I dismissed forever my charnel apprehensions. Alas! the grim legion of sepulchral terrors cannot be regarded as altogether fanciful, but they must sleep, or they will devour us—they must be suffered to slumber, or we perish.

What relationship had their two children to one another?

THE
PREMATURE
BURIAL

37

Solution on page 206

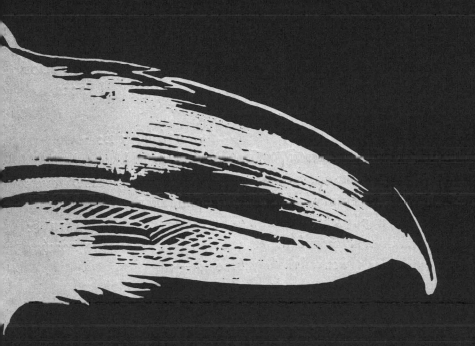

THE
RAVEN

A Visitor From Acheron

Once upon a midnight dreary, while I pondered, weak and weary,
Over many a quaint and curious volume of forgotten lore,
While I nodded, nearly napping, suddenly there came a tapping,
As of some one gently rapping, rapping at my chamber door.
"Tis some visitor", I muttered, "tapping at my chamber door-
Only this, and nothing more."

Startled by the nearing figure, here I longed for pistol trigger,
As each ghastly mental glimmer topped the visions that came before.
My eyes adjusted to the night in time for a **malignant** sight:
A man, rawboned, ablush with spite, stood waiting at my chamber door-
Stood waiting, this Charon, under the bust above my chamber door-
Stood and stared and nothing more.

Increasingly I grew confused - the things he said, the words he used-
About a riddle and his cruel gambit, lingering in store.
"I have a single eye", he shared, "yet cannot see, even if dared.
Your grimace says you should be scared as I am used to human gore."
The answer fled with my courage, now, as I could think only of gore.
I was done, for evermore.

"I have a single eye, yet cannot see." What is he?

THE
RAVEN

40

THE
RAVEN

41

Solution on page 207

THE
RAVEN

42

A Murder Of Crows

Open here I flung the shutter, when, with many a flirt and flutter,
In there stepped a stately Raven of the saintly days of yore;
Not the least obeisance made he; not a minute stopped or stayed he;
But, with mien of lord or lady, perched above my chamber door—
Perched upon a bust of Pallas just above my chamber door—
Perched, and sat, and nothing more.

Then this ebony bird beguiling my sad fancy into smiling,
By the grave and stern decorum of the countenance it wore,
"Though thy crest be shorn and shaven, thou," I said, "art sure no craven,
Ghastly grim and ancient Raven wandering from the Nightly shore—
Tell me what thy lordly name is on the Night's Plutonian shore!"
Quoth the Raven: "Nevermore."

Much I marvelled this ungainly fowl to hear discourse so plainly,
Though its answer little meaning—little relevancy bore;
"I saw foul crows once, eighty, all cawing jointly in a beech tree,
And with my musket weighty shot one dead as a studded nail
within a door—
Answer what number were left or become as a studded nail in a door!"
Quoth the Raven: "Nevermore."

What number were left?

THE
RAVEN

43

Solution on page 207

But the Raven, sitting lonely on the placid bust, spoke only
That one word, as if his soul in that one word he did outpour.
Nothing farther then he uttered—not a feather then he fluttered—
Till I scarcely more than muttered "Other friends have flown before—
On the morrow he will leave me, as my Hopes have flown before."
Then the bird said: "Nevermore."

Startled at the stillness broken by reply so aptly spoken,
"Doubtless," said I, "what it utters is its only stock and store
Caught from some unhappy master whom unmerciful Disaster
Followed fast and followed faster till his songs one burden bore—
Till the dirges of his Hope that melancholy burden bore
Of 'Never—nevermore.'"

But the Raven still beguiling all my fancy into smiling,
Straight I wheeled a cushioned seat in front of bird, and bust and door;
"It is true that forward I am heavy, enough to strain a levee,
As if several, perhaps a bevy, of rooks did cluster atop a sycamore—
Another corvid flock to shame me, did cluster atop a sycamore.
Yet backwards I am not, I am nothing more."

"What am I?"

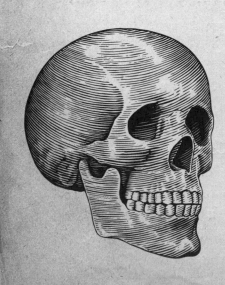

THE
RAVEN

44

THE
RAVEN

45

Solution on page 207

Balm In Gilead

"Prophet!" said I, "thing of evil!—prophet still, if bird or devil!
By that Heaven that bends above us—by that God we both adore—
Why is it that the fowl least craven is the grim and ancient Raven
A creature gaunt yet most brave when its fiery eyes burn into
my bosom's core;
A creature desolate yet all undaunted when its fiery eyes burn
into my bosom's core;
Quoth the Raven: "Nevermore."

"Be that word our sign of parting, bird or fiend!" I shrieked, upstarting—
"Get thee back into the tempest and the Night's Plutonian shore!
Leave no black plume as a token of that lie thy soul hath spoken!
Leave my loneliness unbroken!—quit the bust above my door!
Take thy beak from out my heart, and take thy form from off my door!"
Quoth the Raven: "Nevermore."

And the Raven, never flitting, still is sitting, **still** is sitting
On the pallid bust of Pallas just above my chamber door;
And his eyes have all the seeming of a demon's that is dreaming,
And the lamp-light o'er him streaming throws his shadow on the floor;
And my soul from out that shadow that lies floating on the floor
Shall be lifted—nevermore!

THE
RAVEN

46

Why is it that the fowl
least craven is the grim
and ancient Raven?

THE
RAVEN

47

Solution on page 207

All The Jewels Of Golconda Awaiting

The *Gold-Bug* was the most popular of Edgar Allan Poe's short stories published during his lifetime. Capitalising on the mid-19th century vogue for cryptography, the story features its protagonist William Legrand solving the substitution cipher in the passage below to find a treasure buried by the legendary pirate Captain Kidd.

In Poe's story, Legrand explains the methodology for solving the cipher at great length, but can you decode the message without help? The cipher is in English and does not include breaks or other punctuation, and it helps to ascertain the predominant letters as well as the least frequent.

"Have you ever heard of any important treasure being unearthed along the coast?"

"Never".

"Kidd's accumulations were immense, is well known. I took it for granted, therefore, that the earth still held them; and you will scarcely be surprised when I tell you that I felt a hope, nearly amounting to certainty, that the parchment so strangely found, involved a lost record of the place of deposit. I held the vellum again to the fire, after increasing the heat; but nothing appeared. I now thought it possible that the coating of dirt might have something to do with the failure; so I carefully rinsed the parchment by pouring warm water over it, and, having done this, I placed it in a tin pan and put the pan upon a furnace of lighted charcoal. In a few minutes, the pan having become thoroughly heated, I removed the slip, and, to my inexpressible joy, found it spotted with what appeared to be figures arranged in lines. Again I placed it in the pan, and suffered it to remain another minute. On taking it off, the whole was just as you see it now."

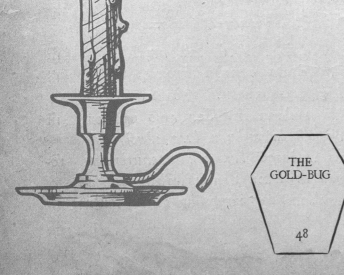

THE
GOLD-BUG

Here Legrand, having re-heated the parchment, submitted it to my inspection. The following characters were rudely traced, in a red tint:

"But," said I, returning him the slip, "I am as much in the dark as ever. Were all the jewels of Golconda awaiting me on my solution of this enigma, I am quite sure that I should be unable to earn them".

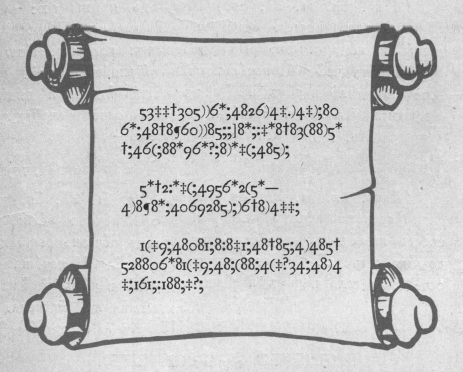

53‡‡†305))6*;4826)4‡.)4‡);80
6*;48†8¶60))85;;]8*;:‡*8†83(88)5*
†;46(;88*96*?;8)*‡(;485);

5*†2:*‡(;4956*2(5*—
4)8¶8*;4069285);)6†8)4‡‡;

1(‡9;48081;8:8‡1;48†85;4)485†
528806*81(‡9;48;(88;4(‡?34;48)4
‡;161;:188;‡?;

Can you decode the message without help?

THE
GOLD-BUG

49

Solution on page 207

The Propensity for Perversity

Phrenologists, in the consideration of the faculties of the human soul, have failed to make room for a propensity which has been equally overlooked by all the moralists who preceded them. In the pure arrogance of reason, we have all overlooked it. We saw no **need** of the impulse. The intellectual man, rather than the observant man, dictated purposes to God, establishing every thing from the preconceived destiny of man. It would have been wiser to classify upon the basis of what man usually did rather than upon what we assumed the Deity intended him to do. Induction would have brought phrenology to admit an innate and primitive principle of human action, which, for want of a more characteristic term, we may call **perverseness**.

In the sense I intend, perverseness is a reason without motive. Through its promptings we act without comprehensible object, we act for the reason that we should **not**. In theory, no reason can be more unreasonable; but, in fact, there is none more strong.

With certain minds, under certain conditions, it becomes absolutely irresistible. The wrongness of any action is the one unconquerable force which impels us to its prosecution. We have a task before us which must be speedily performed. We know that it will be ruinous to make delay. The most important crisis of our life calls, trumpet-tongued, for immediate energy and action. We glow, consumed with eagerness to commence the work, with the anticipation of whose glorious result our whole souls are on fire. I can accomplish this task in two hours, my close acquaintance can do likewise in three hours, and his son would be able to do it in six. It must, **it shall** be undertaken today, and yet we put it off until tomorrow; and why? There is no answer, except that we feel **perverse**.

THE IMP
OF THE
PERVERSE

50

Tomorrow arrives, and with it a more impatient **anxiety** to do our duty, but with this also arrives a nameless, unfathomable craving for delay. This craving gathers strength as the moments fly. The last hour for action is at hand. We tremble with the violence of the conflict within us. The clock strikes, and is the knell of our welfare. It flies— it disappears—we are free. The old energy returns. We will labour **now**. Alas, it is **too late!**

How long would it have taken the three of us to accomplish the task together?

THE IMP
OF THE
PERVERSE

51

Solution on page 208

A single thought is enough. The impulse increases to a wish, the wish to a desire, the **desire** to an uncontrollable longing, and the longing—to the deep regret and mortification of the individual, and in defiance of all consequences—is indulged.

We stand upon the brink of a precipice. The top of a steeple, say, in a town where we know no-one. We peer down—we grow sick and dizzy. Our first impulse is to shrink from the danger. Unaccountably we remain. By slow degrees our sickness and dizziness become merged in a cloud of unnamable feeling.

We think of how we approached this place with our staff, five feet long, and how it cast a three-foot-long shadow. It is the same hour and the steeple casts a shadow that is 120 feet long, thus even the idle contemplation of the steeple's height makes one feel ill.

By gradations, still more imperceptible, the cloud assumes a shape far more terrible than any **demon** of a tale, and yet it is but a thought, one which chills the very marrow of our bones with the fierceness of the delight of its horror. It is the idea of what would be our sensations during a fall from such a height.

And this fall—this rushing annihilation—for the very reason that it involves all those most ghastly and loathsome images of death and suffering which have ever presented themselves to our imagination—for this very cause do we now most vividly desire it. There is no passion in nature so demoniacally impatient, as that of him who, shuddering upon the edge of a precipice, thus meditates a plunge.

How tall is the steeple? Surely we must find out for ourselves. If there be no friendly arm to check us, or if we fail in a sudden effort to prostrate ourselves backward from the abyss, we plunge, and are destroyed.

How tall is the steeple?

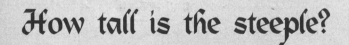

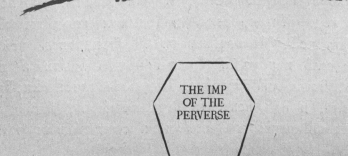

THE IMP
OF THE
PERVERSE

53

Solution on page 208

Extinguishing a Flame

I have said much so that in some measure I may answer your question—that I may explain to you why I am here—that I may assign to you something that shall have at least the faint aspect of a cause for my tenanting this cell of the **condemned**. Had I not been thus drawn out, you might either have misunderstood me altogether, or, with the rabble, have fancied me mad. As it is, you will easily perceive that I am one of the many uncounted victims of the Imp of the Perverse.

It is impossible that any deed could have been wrought with a more thorough deliberation. For months I pondered upon the means of the murder. I rejected a thousand schemes because their accomplishment involved a *chance* of detection. At length, in reading some French memoirs, I found an account of a nearly fatal illness that occurred through the agency of a candle accidentally poisoned.

THE IMP
OF THE
PERVERSE

The idea struck my fancy at once. I knew my victim's habit of reading in bed. I knew, too, that his apartment was narrow and ill-ventilated. But I need not vex you with impertinent details. I need not describe the easy artifices by which I substituted, in his bed-room candle-stand, two wax-lights of my own making for the ones which I there found—one which would burn for four hours and the other for five, just to be sure.

The next morning he was discovered dead in his bed, and the coroner's verdict was: "Death by the visitation of God." I presume that my victim had attempted to extinguish the candles as he writhed in his death agonies, for when I arrived the following day, hoping to silently admire my grim work, I observed that what remained of one wax-light was exactly four times the length of what was left of the other.

How long did it take for him to die? I asked myself, but I understood that any answer would be both too long and too short for my liking.

How long did it take for him to die?

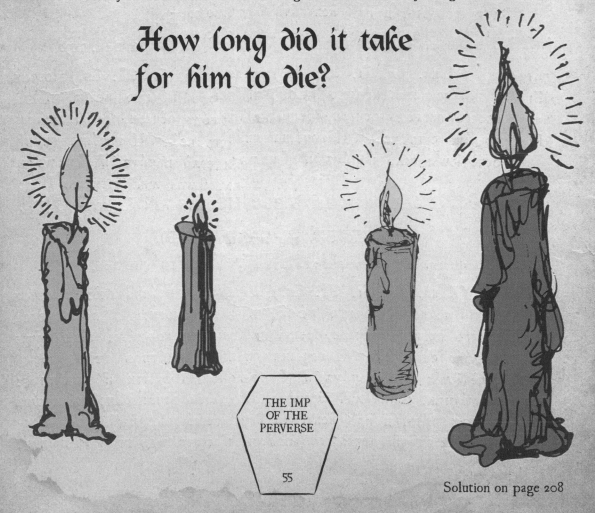

THE IMP
OF THE
PERVERSE

Solution on page 208

If I Be Not Fool Enough

Having inherited my victim's estate, all went well for years.
The idea of detection never once entered my brain. Of the remains of the
fatal taper I had myself carefully disposed. I had left no shadow of a
clue by which it would be possible to convict, or even to suspect,
me of the crime. It is inconceivable how rich my satisfaction
was as I reflected upon my absolute security. For a very
long period of time I was accustomed to revel in this
sentiment. It afforded me more real delight than all
the mere worldly advantages accruing from my sin.
But there arrived at length an epoch, from which
the pleasurable feeling grew into a **haunting** and
harassing thought. I would perpetually catch myself
pondering upon my security, and repeating, in a
low under-tone, "I am safe."

One day, whilst sauntering along the streets,
I arrested myself in the act of murmuring these
customary syllables. In a fit of petulance,
I re-modelled them thus: " I am safe—I am
safe—yes—if I be not fool enough to make
open confession!" No sooner had I spoken
these words, than I felt an icy chill creep to
my heart. I had some experience in these fits
of perversity, and I remembered well that in no
instance I had successfully resisted their attacks.

THE IMP
OF THE
PERVERSE

And now my own casual self-suggestion, that I might possibly be fool
enough to confess the murder of which I had been guilty, confronted me,
as if the very ghost of him whom I had murdered—and beckoned
me on to death. I felt a maddening desire to shriek aloud. I bounded
like a madman through the crowded thoroughfares, thinking
ruefully of the old enigma, "why is a man committing murder
like a hen walking across the street?"

I felt then the consummation of my fate. Could I have
torn out my tongue, I would have done it. Some invisible
fiend, I thought, struck me with his broad palm upon
the back. The long-imprisoned secret burst forth
from my soul, as if in dread of interruption before
concluding the brief but pregnant sentences that
consigned me to the hangman and to hell. But why
shall I say more? To-day I wear these chains,
and am here! Tomorrow I shall be fetterless!—
but where?

"Why is a man committing murder like a hen walking across the street?"

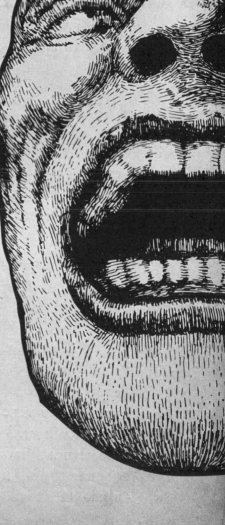

THE IMP
OF THE
PERVERSE

Solution on page 208

THE PIT AND THE PENDULUM

THE PIT
AND THE
PENDULUM

60

I was sick—sick unto death with that long agony; and when they at length unbound me, and I was permitted to sit, I felt that my senses were leaving me. The sentence—the dread sentence of death—was the last of distinct accentuation which reached my ears. After that, the sound of the inquisitorial voices seemed merged in one dreamy indeterminate hum. Until that moment, the judges' torture had assumed a more mundane composition. They explained that two slips of paper had been placed into a receptacle, one marked "DEATH" and the other marked "PARDON". This, perhaps, was the cruellest joke of all, for I knew that both pieces of paper had been marked with "DEATH". It wasn't until after I had failed their test and given them the paper that bore the imprimatur of the grave that I understood what I should have done differently.

What could I have done to secure my freedom?

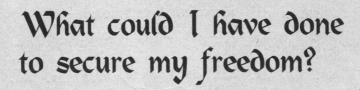

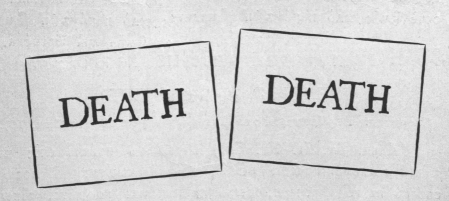

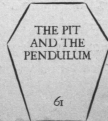

THE PIT
AND THE
PENDULUM

61

Solution on page 209

Presently I heard no more, yet, for a while, I saw; but with how terrible an exaggeration! I saw the lips of the black-robed judges. They appeared to me white—whiter than the sheet upon which I trace these words—and thin even to grotesqueness; thin with the intensity of their expression of firmness—of immoveable resolution—of stern contempt of human torture. I saw that the decrees of what to me was Fate were still issuing from those lips. I saw them writhe with a deadly locution. I saw them fashion the syllables of my name; and I shuddered because no sound succeeded.

After failing the first opportunity, I was offered another, although I knew that this, too, was just a way to prolong my suffering. Two jars were placed in front of me. I was informed that one contained a hundred red marbles and the other contained a hundred black ones. I was free to redistribute the marbles however I wished, and when I was done the jars would be thoroughly shaken. At that point I would be blindfolded and presented with one at random. To be pardoned, I would have to pull a red marble out of the jar—a black marble, of course, would mean my death.

I followed the judges' pitiless request and was profoundly unsurprised to learn that I had failed once more: the marble I pulled out was black as the judges' hearts. The question took lodgings in my head, torturing me:

How should I have distributed the marbles to have the best chance of being set free?

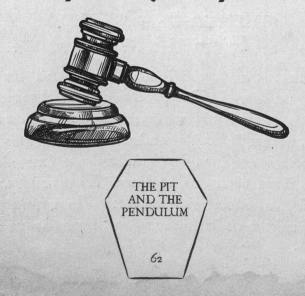

THE PIT
AND THE
PENDULUM

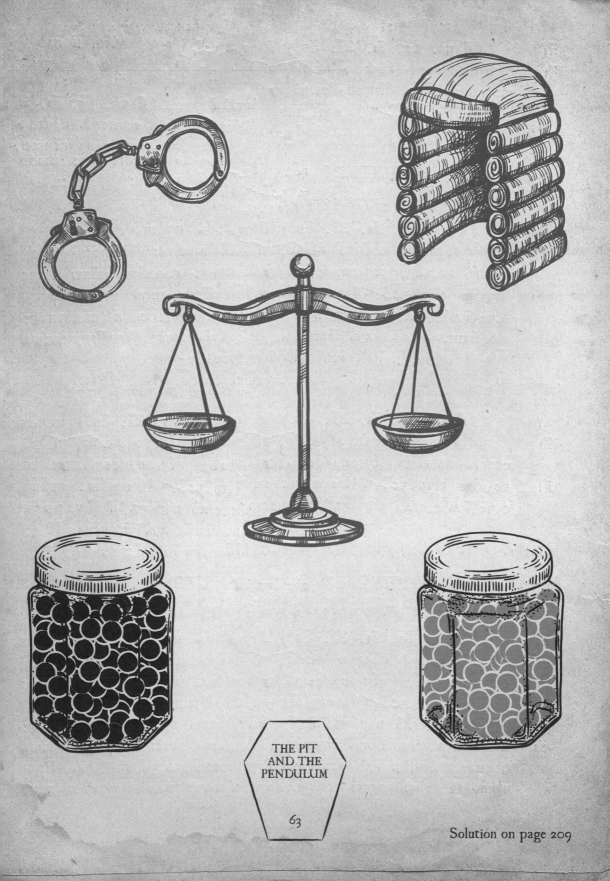

THE PIT
AND THE
PENDULUM

63

Solution on page 209

The thought stole into my fancy, like a rich musical note, of what sweet rest there must be in the grave. This notion came gently and stealthily, and it seemed that a long period passed before it attained full appreciation; but just as my spirit came at length properly to feel and entertain it, the figures of the judges vanished, as if magically, from before me; the tall candles sank into nothingness; their flames went out utterly; the blackness of **darkness** supervened; all sensations appeared swallowed up in a mad rushing descent as of the soul into Hades. Then silence, stillness and night were the universe.

I had swooned. Very suddenly there came back to my soul motion and sound—the tumultuous motion of the heart, and, in my ears, the sound of its beating. Then a pause in which all is blank. Then again sound, and motion, and touch—a tingling sensation pervading my frame. I awoke to see nine individuals, each as wretched as I, lined up in a row ahead of me. Each prisoner faced the same direction, only able to see the people ahead of them. A judge announced that he would place either a red or a black hat on each person's head, choosing any arrangement and number of hats. This meant, naturally, that each person could only see the colour of the hats in front.

The judge explained his plan to move from the back to the front of the line, asking each prisoner in turn, myself included, what colour hat they were wearing—a question they could only answer with the words "red" or "black". If the prisoner replied correctly they would be released, and if they replied incorrectly then they would die. We were granted a few moments to devise a plan of action as the judges watched with their cold eyes. They wanted us to fail and we did, for none of us could agree on the answer to the question:

What could be done in order to maximize the number of prisoners that would be released?

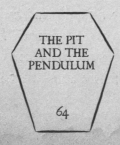

THE PIT
AND THE
PENDULUM

64

Solution on page 209

Upon recovering, I at once started to my feet, trembling convulsively in every fibre. I thrust my arms wildly above and around me in all directions. I felt nothing; yet dreaded to move a step lest I should be impeded by the walls of a **tomb**. Perspiration burst from every pore, and stood in cold big beads upon my forehead.

The agony of suspense grew at length intolerable, and I cautiously moved forward, with my arms extended, and my eyes straining from their sockets, in the hope of catching some faint ray of light. I proceeded for many paces; but still all was blackness and **vacancy**. As I still continued to step cautiously onward, there came thronging upon my recollection a thousand vague rumours of the horrors of Toledo. Of the dungeons there had been strange things narrated— fables I had always deemed them—but yet strange, and too ghastly to repeat, save in a whisper. Was I left to perish of starvation in this subterranean world of darkness; or what fate, perhaps even more fearful, awaited me?

At long last my outstretched hands encountered some solid obstruction. It was a wall, seemingly of stone masonry— very smooth, slimy, and cold. I followed it up; stepping with all the careful distrust with which certain antique narratives had inspired me. I came to a door, and then another, and then a third, and then a fourth.

On the first door was a sheaf of paper, upon which was written, "The BEAST is behind the second or third door." The note on the second door read, "The BEAST is behind the first or fourth door." The note on the third door read, "The BEAST is HERE," and the note on the fourth door read "The BEAST is not behind this door," I understood that the beast—whatever it was—lay behind one of the doors, and likewise that three of the doors would be lying. "Where is the beast?", I cried to the darkness, but the darkness remained silent.

"Where is the beast?"

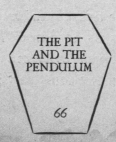

THE PIT
AND THE
PENDULUM

THE PIT
AND THE
PENDULUM

67

Solution on page 210

A Dark And Final Abyss

Quitting the wall, I resolved to cross the area of the enclosure. At first
I proceeded with extreme caution, for the floor, although seemingly of
solid material, was treacherous with slime. I had advanced some ten or
twelve paces in this manner when the remnant of the torn hem of my robe
became entangled between my legs. I stepped on it and fell violently on
my face. My chin rested upon the floor of the prison, but my lips and the
upper portion of my head, although seemingly at a less elevation than the
chin, touched nothing. At the same time my forehead seemed bathed in
a clammy vapour, and the peculiar smell of decayed fungus arose to my
nostrils. I put forward my arm, and shuddered to find that I had fallen at
the very brink of a circular pit, whose extent, of course, I had no means
of ascertaining.

Groping about the masonry just below the margin, I succeeded in
dislodging a small fragment, and let it fall. For many seconds I hearkened
to its reverberations as it dashed against the sides of the chasm in its
descent. I saw clearly the doom which had been prepared for me: another
step, and the world had seen me no more. I tried to speak, but the
words would not come. I stared down at the hole. "Holes," I whispered,
remembering the enigma my mother had once taught me:

"I am nothing but holes tied to holes, yet I am as strong as iron. What am I?"

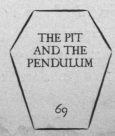

THE PIT
AND THE
PENDULUM

69

Solution on page 210

The death just avoided was of that very character which I had regarded as fabulous and frivolous in the tales relating the Inquisition. To its victims, there was the choice of death with its direst physical agonies or death with its most hideous moral horrors. I had been reserved for the latter.

My long suffering my nerves had been unstrung, until I trembled at the sound of my own voice, and had become in every respect a fitting subject for the species of torture which awaited me. Shaking in every limb, I groped my way back to the wall, resolving there to perish rather than risk the terrors of the wells, of which my imagination now pictured many in various positions about the **dungeon**.

In other conditions of mind I might have had courage to end my misery at once by a plunge into one of the abysses; but now I was the veriest of cowards. Neither could I forget what I had read of these pits—that the sudden extinction of life formed no part of their most horrible plan.

I found, with grim inevitability, that there was yet another set of doors ahead of me. I felt sure that these had not been apparent before, which meant that either my senses had abandoned me or I was being watched at that precise moment.

The note on the first door read, "There is a pit behind this door" and "the safe door will lead into a slightly smaller room."

THE PIT
AND THE
PENDULUM

70

The note on the second, meanwhile, stated, "There is a pit behind the first door," and "the safe door will lead into a slightly larger room." The note on the third door read, "This door leads to a pit," and "The first or second door is really the safe one." Having learned more than I would have liked about the **cunning** of my tormentors, I understood that each door would surely contain no more than one false statement. I stood frozen, unable to make my simple, very likely catastrophic decision:

Which door should I take?

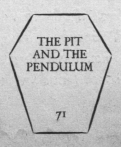

THE PIT
AND THE
PENDULUM

71

Solution on page 210

The Gathering Squall

Bound to a low framework of wood, I surveyed the ceiling of my prison: the painted figure of Time, in lieu of a scythe, held a huge pendulum such as we see on antique clocks. Its sweep, thirty feet overhead, was brief and of course slow. I watched it for some minutes, somewhat in fear, but more in wonder. Wearied at length with observing its dull movement, I turned my attention upon the other objects in the cell.

Half an hour dripped away before I again cast my eyes upward. What I saw confounded and amazed me. The pendulum had perceptibly descended by a yard. Its sweep had increased in extent and as a consequence its velocity was also much greater. I now observed—with what horror it is needless to say—that its nether extremity was formed of a crescent of glittering steel a foot in length from horn to horn, and the under edge evidently as keen as a **razor**. The vibration of the pendulum was at right angles to my length. I saw that the crescent was designed to cross the region of the heart. It would fray the serge of my robe, returning to repeat its operations again and again.

I could no longer doubt the doom prepared for me by monkish ingenuity in torture. I knew that surprise, or entrapment into **torment**, formed an important portion of all the grotesquerie of these dungeon deaths. Having failed to fall into the pit, it was no part of the demon plan to hurl me into the abyss; and thus a different and a milder destruction awaited me. Milder! I half smiled in my agony as I thought of such application of such a term. I began to deduce how long it would take for the pendulum to smite me, and my despair was not soothed by the knowledge that I had some time to figure it out.

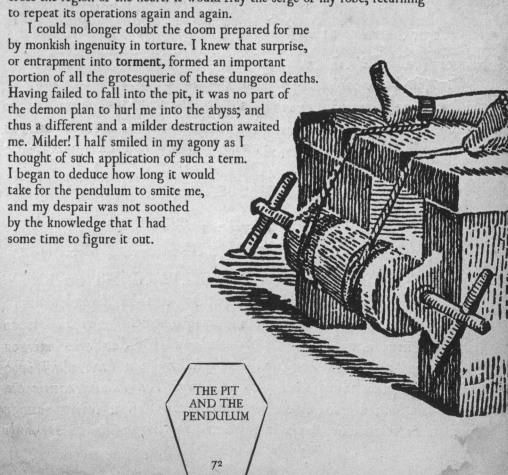

THE PIT
AND THE
PENDULUM

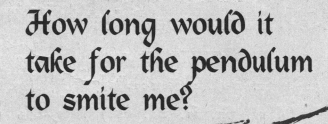

How long would it take for the pendulum to smite me?

THE PIT
AND THE
PENDULUM

73

Solution on page 210

Up In Flames

Forth from the well the rats hurried in fresh troops. They clung to the wood—they overran it, and leaped in hundreds upon my person. The measured movement of the pendulum disturbed them not at all. Avoiding its strokes they busied themselves with gnawing at my bandages. They were wild, bold, ravenous; their red eyes glaring upon me as if they waited but for motionlessness on my part to make me their prey.

"To what food," I thought, "have they been accustomed?" They swarmed upon me in ever accumulating heaps. They writhed upon my throat; their cold lips sought my own; I was half stifled by their thronging pressure; disgust, for which the world has no name, swelled my bosom, and chilled, with a heavy clamminess, my heart. Yet one minute, and I felt that the struggle would be over, and I would be free. The stroke of the pendulum already pressed upon my bosom, but the moment of escape had arrived. With a steady movement—cautious, sidelong, shrinking, and slow—I slid beyond the reach of the scimitar. For the moment, at least, I was free.

Free—and in the grasp of the Inquisition! I had scarcely stepped upon the stone floor of the prison when the motion of the hellish machine ceased and I beheld it drawn up, by some invisible force, through the ceiling. I rolled my eyes nervously around on the barriers of iron that hemmed me in. There came to my nostrils the breath of the vapour of heated iron.

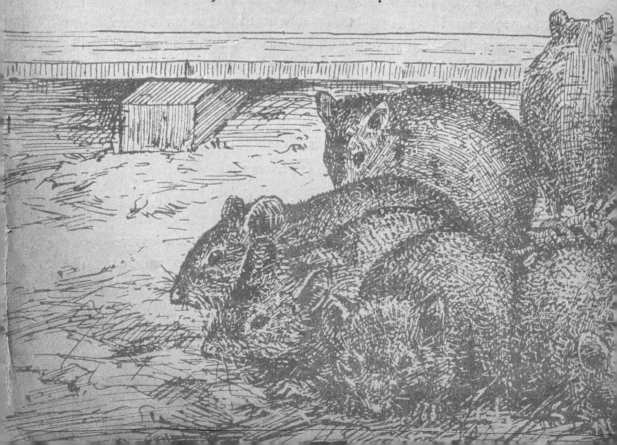

Solution on page 210

There could be no doubt of the design of my **tormentors**—oh! most unrelenting! oh! most demoniac of men! I had but escaped death in one form of agony, to be delivered unto worse than death in some other. After everything, I would be burned alive. Oh!—horror!—any horror but this!

That a rope would be suddenly and dramatically loosened from its fixture was surely an unintended consequence of the heat. The end of the rope, just touching the ground, led right up to the ceiling and my potential freedom. At rest, the rope was four feet from the enkindled wall, but as I pulled it to the wall, keeping it taut, it touched a point three inches above the floor. In the circumstances I knew I would be barely able to climb at all, but estimated I'd be able to endure about 40 feet before I succumbed to the fumes and fell to my doom.

"Would I be able to escape?" I tried not to ask myself, yet I could think of nothing else, except, perhaps, the rats.

"Would I be able to escape?"

THE PIT
AND THE
PENDULUM

75

Brilliant But Unlicensed

Edgar Allan Poe often wrote anonymously for publications on a range of subjects, which can cause complications in correctly identifying his work. The literature professor Thomas Ollive Mabbott identified the poem below, signed only with the letter "P", as being the anonymous effort of Poe.

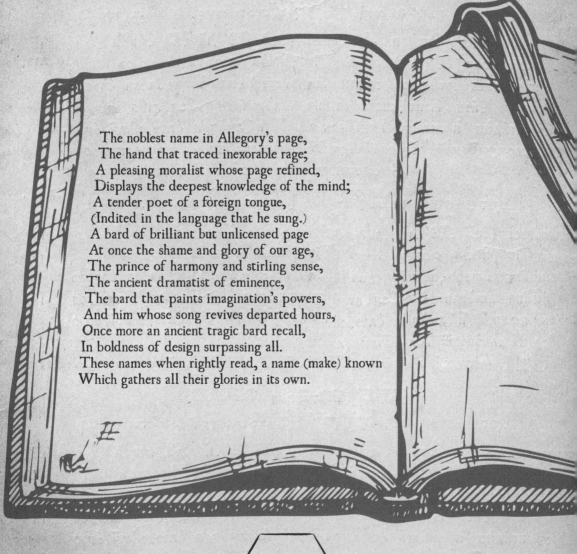

The noblest name in Allegory's page,
The hand that traced inexorable rage;
A pleasing moralist whose page refined,
Displays the deepest knowledge of the mind;
A tender poet of a foreign tongue,
(Indited in the language that he sung.)
A bard of brilliant but unlicensed page
At once the shame and glory of our age,
The prince of harmony and stirling sense,
The ancient dramatist of eminence,
The bard that paints imagination's powers,
And him whose song revives departed hours,
Once more an ancient tragic bard recall,
In boldness of design surpassing all.
These names when rightly read, a name (make) known
Which gathers all their glories in its own.

ENIGMA

The poem, which appeared in the February 2, 1833 issue of the *Baltimore Saturday Visiter*, refers to eleven literary figures. Mabbott also went to the trouble of attempting to solve the puzzle.

Can you figure out which writers he believed Poe was referring to?

ENIGMA

77

Solution on page 211

A Horrible Improbability

Of course I shall not pretend to consider it any matter for wonder that the **extraordinary** case of M. Valdemar has excited discussion. It would have been a miracle had it not. Through the desire of all parties concerned to keep the affair from the public—at least until we had farther opportunities for investigation—a garbled or exaggerated account made its way into society, and became the source of many unpleasant misrepresentations, and, very naturally, of a great deal of disbelief. It is now rendered necessary that I give the **facts**—as far as I comprehend them. They are, succinctly, these:

My attention, for the last three years, had been repeatedly drawn to the subject of Mesmerism; and, about nine months ago, it occurred to me, quite suddenly, that in the series of experiments made hitherto, there had been a remarkable and unaccountable omission: no person had as yet been mesmerised in **articulo mortis**. It remained to be seen whether, in such condition, there existed in the patient any susceptibility to the magnetic influence, or to what extent the encroachments of Death might be arrested by the process.

In looking for some subject by whose means I might test these particulars, I was brought to think of my friend, M. Ernest Valdemar. His temperament was markedly nervous, and rendered him a good subject for mesmeric experiment. His keen intellect also marked him out; lately I had taken to posing conundrums to influenced patients.

In reawakening a crucial part of their dormant mind, I hypothesised, a precisely-chosen enigma would allow me access to the rest of it. For instance, on my first attempt at this procedure, I asked my patient the following:

THE FACTS
IN THE
CASE OF M.
VALDEMAR

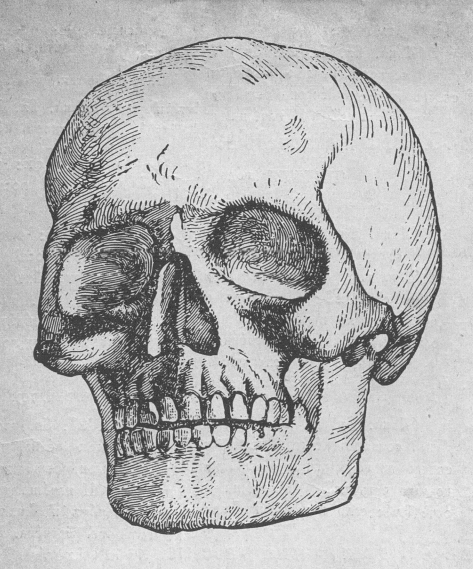

"What's the difference between dead soldiers and repaired garments?"

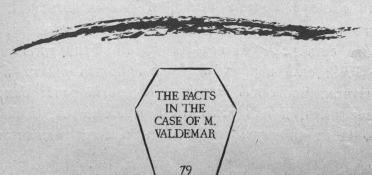

THE FACTS
IN THE
CASE OF M.
VALDEMAR

79

Solution on page 211

On two or three occasions I had put M. Valdemar to sleep with little difficulty, but was disappointed in other results which his peculiar constitution had naturally led me to anticipate. His will was at no period positively, or thoroughly, under my control, and in regard to **clairvoyance**, I could accomplish with him nothing to be relied upon. I always attributed my failure at these points not to his mind but to the disordered state of his health. For some months previous to my becoming acquainted with him, his physicians had diagnosed him with tuberculosis. When the ideas to which I have alluded first occurred to me, it was natural that I should think of M. Valdemar. I knew the steady philosophy of the man too well to apprehend any scruples from him; and he had no relatives in America who would be likely to interfere. I spoke to him frankly upon the subject; and, to my surprise, his interest seemed vividly excited. His disease was of that character which would admit of exact calculation in respect to the epoch of its termination in **death**; and it was finally arranged between us that he would send for me a day before the period announced by his physicians as that of his decease. During the seven months that followed I met up with him on several occasions for trial procedures, but they were only a partial success. The mesmerism attempts lacked for improvement, except for when he responded—albeit with no small annoyance—upon my asking of the question:

"A train leaves from Annapolis to Rockwood along the Baltimore & Ohio rail-road. An hour later, another one leaves from Rockwood to Annapolis. The two engines are moving at exactly the same speed, so:

Which train will be nearer to Rockwood when they meet?"

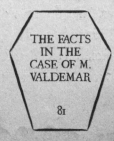

THE FACTS
IN THE
CASE OF M.
VALDEMAR

Solution on page 211

"You may as well come now. I cannot hold out beyond to-morrow midnight."

I received the note half an hour after it was written, and in fifteen minutes more I was in the dying man's chamber. I was appalled by the fearful alteration which the brief interval had wrought in him. His face wore a leaden hue; the eyes were utterly lustreless; and the emaciation was so extreme that the skin had been broken through by the cheek-bones. He retained, nevertheless, his mental power, and when I entered the room he still professed himself quite anxious to have the experiment made, and urged me to begin at once. "Yes, I wish to be mesmerized," he said feebly, "I fear you have deferred it too long."

While he spoke thus, I commenced the passes which I had already found most effectual in subduing him. As he was already in the death agony, I proceeded without hesitation, directing my gaze entirely into his right eye. By this time his pulse was imperceptible and his breathing was stertorous, a condition that was nearly unaltered for a quarter of an hour. At the expiration of this period, however, a natural but deep sigh escaped the bosom of the dying man, and the breathing ceased.

At five minutes before eleven I perceived unequivocal signs of the mesmeric influence. The glassy roll of the eyes was changed for that expression of uneasy inward examination which is only seen in cases of sleep-waking, and which is quite impossible to mistake. With a few rapid lateral passes I made the lids quiver, as in incipient sleep, and with a few more I closed them altogether. He was in an unusually perfect state of mesmeric trance; thus I felt confident in awakening his dormant mind.

"Three men met on the street," I asked, oblivious of the hornet's nest I was prodding, "Mr. Yellow, Mr. White and Mr. Black. 'Are you aware', asked Mr. White, 'that between us we are wearing yellow, white and black, and yet not one of us is wearing the colour of his name?' 'My word, you're right!' said the man in yellow.

Which man was wearing which colour?"

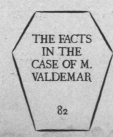

THE FACTS
IN THE
CASE OF M.
VALDEMAR

Solution on page 211

"M. Valdemar," I said, "are you asleep?" He made no answer, but I perceived a tremor about the lips, and was induced to repeat the question, again and again. I did not think it advisable to disturb him farther just then. It was now the opinion, or rather the wish, of his physicians, that M. Valdemar should be suffered to remain undisturbed in his present tranquil condition, until death should supervene—and this, it was generally agreed, must now take place within a few minutes. I concluded, however, to speak to him once more, and merely repeated my previous question.

While I spoke, there came a marked change over the countenance of the sleep-waker. The eyes rolled themselves slowly open, the pupils disappearing upwardly; the skin generally assumed a cadaverous hue. It put me in mind of nothing so much as the extinguishment of a candle by a puff of the **breath**. The upper lip, at the same time, writhed itself away from the teeth, which it had previously covered completely; while the lower jaw fell with an inaudible jerk, leaving the mouth widely extended, and disclosing in full view the swollen and blackened tongue. I now feel that I have reached a point of this narrative at which every reader will be startled into positive disbelief. It is my business, however, simply to proceed. There was no longer the faintest sign of vitality in M. Valdemar; and concluding him to be dead, we were consigning him to the charge of the nurses, when a strong vibratory motion was observable in the tongue. There issued from the distended and motionless jaws a hideous voice—such as it would be madness in me to attempt describing for the simple reason that no similar sounds have ever jarred upon the ear of **humanity**.

M. Valdemar spoke—obviously in reply to the question I had propounded to him a few minutes before. He now said: "Yes;—no;—I have been sleeping—and now—now—I am dead". The nurses immediately left the chamber, and could not be induced to return. Finding myself in a great beyond of my own making, I was unsure of how to proceed, so I posed another enigma.

"A B D O P Q. What is the next letter in this series?" To my astonishment, he answered correctly, the blackened tongue vibrating in his mouth.

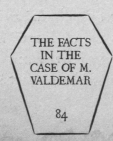

THE FACTS
IN THE
CASE OF M.
VALDEMAR

84

Solution on page 211

What is the
next letter in
this series?

THE FACTS
IN THE
CASE OF M.
VALDEMAR

85

The Living End

I had now some discussion with M. Valdemar's physicians as to the propriety and feasibility of awakening him; but we agreed that no good purpose would be served by so doing. It was evident that, so far, death— or what is usually termed death—had been arrested by the mesmeric process. From this period until the close of last week—an interval of nearly seven months—we continued to make daily calls. All this time the sleep-waker remained **exactly** as I have last described him.

It was on Friday last that we finally resolved to make the experiment of awakening, or attempting to awaken him; and it is the potentially unfortunate result of this latter experiment which has given rise to so much discussion in private circles—to so much of what I cannot help thinking unwarranted popular feeling.

For the purpose of relieving M. Valdemar from the mesmeric trance, I made use of the customary passes. These were unsuccessful. As I had once done so in life and now in death, I suggested an enigma. For a moment, nothing happened, but then the first indication of revival was afforded: a partial descent of the iris. It was observed, as especially remarkable, that this lowering of the pupil was accompanied by the profuse out-flowing of a yellowish **ichor** (from beneath the lids) of a **pungent** and highly offensive odour. The tongue quivered, or rather rolled violently in the mouth (although the jaws and lips remained rigid as before) and at length the same hideous voice which I have already described, broke forth. He answered my question, duly, and then: "For God's sake!— quick!—quick!—put me to sleep—or, quick!—waken me!—quick!— I say to you that I am dead!

I was thoroughly unnerved, and for an instant remained undecided what to do. I retraced my steps and earnestly struggled to awaken him. As I made the mesmeric passes, amid ejaculations of "dead! dead!" absolutely bursting from the tongue and not from the lips of the sufferer, his whole frame at once—within the space of a single minute, or even less, shrunk—crumbled—absolutely rotted away beneath my hands. Upon the bed, before that whole company, there lay a nearly liquid mass of loathsome—of detestable putrescence. I will never forget any of it, nor, indeed, the fateful question that had prompted it:

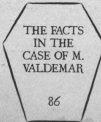

THE FACTS
IN THE
CASE OF M.
VALDEMAR

86

Solution on page 211

"If I drink, I die.
If I eat, I am fine.
What am I?"

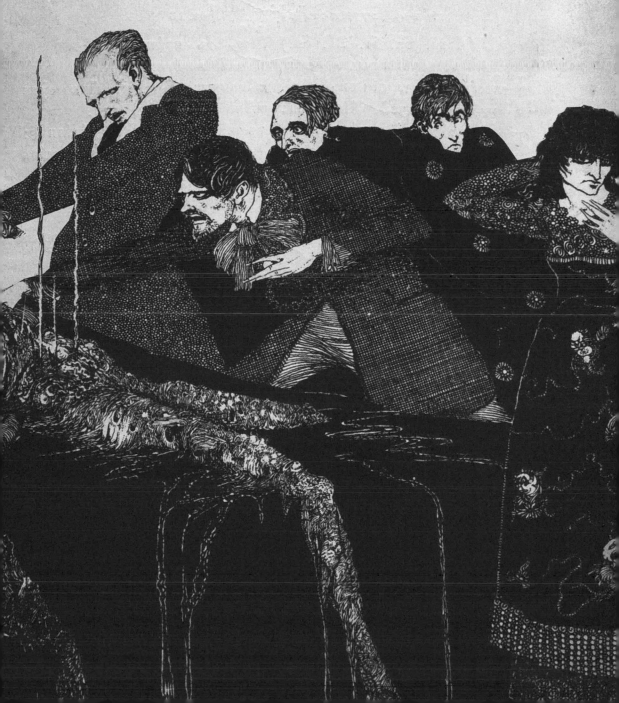

THE
CASK OF
AMONTILLADO

Mistaken May Merrymaking

The thousand injuries of Fortunato I had borne as I best could; but when he ventured upon insult, I vowed revenge. You, who so well know the nature of my soul, will not suppose, however, that I gave utterance to a threat. At length I would be avenged; this was a point definitively settled—but the very definitiveness with which it was resolved, precluded the idea of risk. I must not only punish, but punish with impunity. It must be understood, that neither by word nor deed had I given Fortunato cause to doubt my good-will. I continued, as was my wont, to smile in his face, and he did not perceive that my smile now was at the thought of his immolation.

He had a weak point—this Fortunato—although in other regards he was a man to be respected and even feared. He prided himself on his connoisseurship in wine. In painting and gemmary. Fortunato, like his countrymen, was a quack—but in the matter of old wines he was sincere. In this respect I did not differ from him materially: I was skilful in the Italian vintages myself, and bought largely whenever I could.

It was dusk, one evening during the supreme madness of the carnival, that I encountered my friend. The region's carnival season had long since slipped loose of Lent and could be found roaming through May, its "Mardi Gras" peak held, to the confusion of all, upon the month's second Sunday.

What is the earliest and latest possible date of this Mardi Gras?

THE
CASK OF
AMONTILLADO

THE
CASK OF
AMONTILLADO

91

Solution on page 212

Fortunato accosted me with excessive warmth, for he had been drinking much. The man wore motley. He had on a tight-fitting parti-striped dress and his head was surmounted by the conical cap and bells. I was so pleased to see him that I thought I should never have done wringing his hand.

I said to him: "My dear Fortunato, you are luckily met. How remarkably well you are looking to-day! But I have received a pipe of what passes for Amontillado, and I have my doubts."

"How?" said he. "Amontillado? A pipe? Impossible! And in the middle of the carnival! How much did you pay?"

"I have my doubts," I replied. "I was silly enough to pay the full Amontillado price without consulting you in the matter. I spent three-fourths of my money on the pipe, and then lost three-fourths here paying for the butt to be delivered to my **palazzo**. You were not to be found, and I was fearful of losing a bargain. I only have six lira left."

"Amontillado!"

"How much money did I have to start with? I don't even know."

THE
CASK OF
AMONTILLADO

93

Solution on page 212

"Amontillado!"

"I have my doubts."

"Amontillado!"

"And I must satisfy them."

"Let us go to your vaults!"

" My friend, no; I will not impose upon your good nature. I perceive you have an engagement."

"I have no engagement—come. You have been imposed upon."

Thus speaking, Fortunato possessed himself of my arm, and I suffered him to hurry me to my palazzo. There were no attendants at home; I had told them that I should not return until the morning, and given them explicit orders not to stir from the house. These orders were sufficient, I well knew, to insure their immediate disappearance as soon as my back was turned.

I bowed Fortunato through several suites of rooms to the archway that led into the vaults and down a long and winding staircase, requesting him to be cautious as he followed. We came at length to the foot of the descent and the catacombs of the Montresors. The gait of my friend was unsteady, and the bells upon his cap jingled as he strode. "The pipe?" said he.

"It is farther on," said I, "but a draught of Medoc will gird us."

Here I knocked off the neck of a bottle which I drew from a long row of its fellows. "Drink," I said, presenting him the wine. There were now exactly three bottles of Medoc, three bottles of De Gràve, three bottles of Carnet and three bottles of Dubignon that lay upon the mould.

"If our torches were suddenly extinguished, how many bottles of wine would I have to pick up to ensure that I had at least three of the same type of wine?" I asked.

THE
CASK OF
AMONTILLADO

95

Solution on page 212

Bottle - Bartering Butler

My own fancy grew warm with the Medoc. We had passed through walls of piled bones, with casks and puncheons intermingling, into the inmost recesses of the catacombs. I paused again, and this time I made bold to seize Fortunato by an arm above the elbow.

"Your collection must have cost a fortune," Fortunato remarked. I broke and reached him a **flagon** of De Grave. He emptied it at a breath. His eyes flashed with a fierce light.

"It cost **me** a fortune," I replied. "You are rich, respected, admired, beloved; you are happy, as once I was. You are a man to be missed."

"How much?" He asked, with the slatternly concern of the drunkard.

"I purchased the wine from a merchant who offered a 5% discount. My foremost attendant, however, always receives a 5% commission on my bills, and made this point awkwardly clear. As the merchant only made a profit of 5% on the cost, he raised the bill, which would have been 882 lira if the attendant hadn't intervened."

Fortunato turned toward me, and looked into my eyes with two filmy orbs that distilled the rheum of **intoxication**. He was confused.

THE
CASK OF
AMONTILLADO

96

Solution on page 212

"How much did you pay, then?"

Splitting Stolen Supplies

"You can scream and scream in here and no-one will find you." Fortunato spun around in a circle, looking at his feet.

"It wasn't always so safe, however. Robbers once found there way right here to this exact spot. They took two dozen bottles of my best wine: a dozen demi-bottles and a dozen standard ones. Finding it too heavy to carry, however—or so the local inspector told me—they drank five demi-bottles and five standard bottles to toast their success.

"Hoping to leave no trace to follow, they took the empty bottles with them, but upon arriving at their hideout they discovered that they were unable to fairly divide the seven full bottles and five empty ones and seven demi-bottles and five empty ones so that they each had the same value in bottles and wine. Their quarrels drew the attention of the Public Safety Guards, and that was that. The men somehow 'escaped' before they could be charged. It's astonishing how often criminals escape from our Guards, and how wealthy those Guards seem to be."

I've thought on this matter often.

Without transferring any wine from one bottle to another, as even criminals aren't savages—

THE
CASK OF
AMONTILLADO

98

Solution on page 212

How many robbers were there, and how might they have divided their haul so that each man had an equitable share?"

THE CASK OF AMONTILLADO

99

Fortunato's Family Frustration

Descending again, we arrived at a deep **crypt**, in which the foulness of the air caused our flambeaux rather to glow than flame.

At the most remote end of the crypt there appeared another less spacious. Its walls had been lined with human remains, piled to the vault overhead, in the fashion of the great catacombs of Paris. We perceived a still interior recess; it seemed to have been constructed for no especial use within itself, but formed merely the interval between two of the colossal supports of the roof of the catacombs. It was in vain that Fortunato, uplifting his dull **torch**, endeavoured to pry into the depth of the recess. Its termination the feeble light did not enable us to see.

"My whole family is here in this crypt," I told Fortunato, who was struggling to focus his eyes. "My father. My mother. Her father, her mother. Piruza. Fiordelise. Tortula. There's Onesta, of course, who was Tortula's daughter's aunt's husband's daughter's sister. I could never remember, though: what was the relationship between Onesta and Tortula? Do you know?"

Yet again, Fortunato did not, which was the final signal I needed.

"Never mind. Proceed," I said. "Herein is the Amontillado".

Solution on page 212

What was the relationship between Onesta and Jortula?

THE
CASK OF
AMONTILLADO

101

Callow Crypt Conundrums

Fortunato stepped unsteadily forward, while I followed immediately at his heels. In an instant he had reached the extremity of the niche, and finding his progress arrested by the rock stood stupidly bewildered. A moment more and I had fettered him to the granite. He was too much astounded to resist. "The Amontillado!" exclaimed my friend, not yet recovered from his astonishment.

"True," I replied. "The Amontillado."

As I said these words I began vigorously to wall up the entrance of the niche. I had scarcely laid the first tier of the masonry when I discovered that the intoxication of Fortunato had in a great measure worn off. The earliest indication I had of this was a low moaning cry from the depth of the recess. It was not the cry of a drunken man.

Begging followed screams which followed panicked demands. He asked me what he could do to secure his release from my "very good joke", my "excellent jest". Ask him any question, he said, and he would answer it. I was drawing to the end of the eleventh and last tier. I would indulge him, for his fate was as sealed as the mason soon would be.

"Some try to hide, some try to cheat, but time will show, we always will meet. Try as you might, to guess my name, I promise you'll know when you I do claim—

Who am I?"

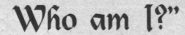

THE
CASK OF
AMONTILLADO

Solution on page 213

A Flight In The Aerial

Astounding News by Express, via Norfolk!—The Atlantic Crossed in Three Days! Signal Triumph of Mr. Monck Mason's Flying Machine!—Arrival at Sullivan's Island, near Charleston, S. C., of Mr. Mason, Mr. R. Holland, Mr. H. Ainsworth, and four others, in the Steering Balloon, "Victoria", after a passage of Seventy-five Hours from Land to Land! Full Particulars of the Voyage!

The great problem is at length solved! The air, as well as the earth and the ocean, has been subdued by science, and will become a common and convenient highway for mankind. The Atlantic has been actually crossed in a Balloon! and this too without difficulty— without any great apparent danger—with thorough control of the machine—and in the inconceivably brief period of seventy-five hours from shore to shore!

By the energy of an agent at Charleston, S.C., we are enabled to be the first to furnish the public with a detailed account of this most extraordinary voyage, which was performed between Saturday the 6th and Tuesday the 9th by Sir Everard Bringhurst; Mr. Osborne, a nephew of Lord Bentinck's; Mr. Monck Mason and Mr. Robert Holland, the well-known aeronauts; Mr. Harrison Ainsworth, author of Jack Sheppard—with two seamen from Woolwich—in all, seven persons.

Two very decided failures, of late—those of Mr. Henson and Sir George Cayley—had much weakened the public interest in the subject of aerial navigation. Mr. Henson's effort was singularly unsuccessful, as his body was found a month later, holding a toothpick and in a state of undress.

What happened to Mr. Henson?

THE
BALLOON
HOAX

104

Solution on page 213

Ruled By A Spiteful Child

I never knew anyone so keenly alive to a joke as the king was. He seemed to live only for joking. To tell a good story of the joke kind, and to tell it well, was the surest road to his favour. Thus it happened that his four ministers were all noted for their accomplishments as jokers. They all took after the king, too, in being large, oily men, as well as inimitable jokers. Whether people grow fat by joking, or whether there is something in fat itself which predisposes to a joke, I have never been quite able to determine; but certain it is that a lean joker is a rare bird in the world.

Of everyone in the court, the ministers were the most likely to evade the king's many tantrums, yet he took great pleasure in giving them insulting nicknames and making them compete against each other physically; this was particularly mean-spirited given that they were each as corpulent as the king himself.

The king had bestowed Flore, Gille, Lanval and Aucassin with the nicknames of Toad, Carbuncle, Turkey brain and Disappointed-his-parents, but not necessarily in that order, and had spent much of several weeks determining that Lanval could run faster than Toad (but couldn't lift as much weight as Turkey brain), Toad was stronger than Aucassin (but slower than Carbuncle), and Flore was faster than both Lanval and Disappointed-his-parents (but not as strong as Toad). The king was thoroughly satisfied by the outcome of this long, strange ordeal, the only problem being that he could no long remember what anyone was called.

HOP-FROG

106

Solution on page 213
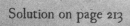

What was the nickname of each minister?

The Ghosts Of Wit

About the refinements, or, as he called them, the "ghosts" of wit, the king troubled himself very little. Upon the whole, practical jokes suited his taste far better than verbal ones. He had an especial admiration for **breadth** in a jest and over-niceties wearied him. Indeed, he only had a single shrewd manoeuvre: the King delighted in shaking new courtiers by their shoulders and squealing the following:

"You! Answer me this grammatical conundrum, or you'll be marching towards the scaffold!

Is it more correct to say the yolk *is* white or the yolk *are* white?"

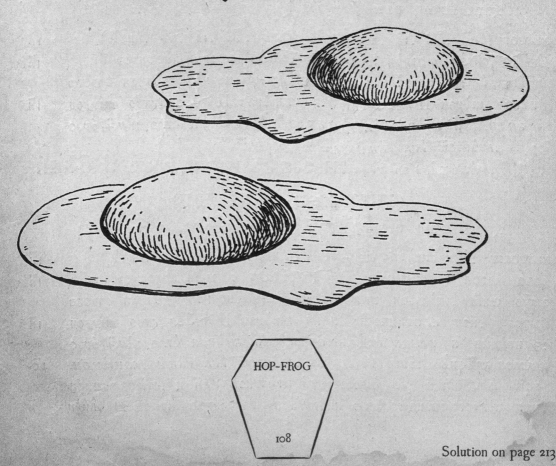

HOP-FROG

108

Solution on page 213

At the date of my narrative, professing jesters had not altogether gone out of fashion at court. Several of the great continental powers still retained their "fools", who wore motley, with caps and bells, and were expected to be always ready with sharp witticisms at a moment's notice, in consideration of the crumbs that fell from the royal table.

Our king, as a matter of course, retained his "fool". The name "Hop-Frog" was not that given to the crippled jester by his sponsors at baptism, but was conferred upon him, by general consent of the seven ministers, on account of his inability to walk as other men do. I am not able to say, with precision, from what country Hop-Frog originally came, but he had been forcibly carried from his home and sent as a present to the king by one of his ever-victorious generals.

Hop-Frog, who, although he made a great deal of sport, was by no means popular, nevertheless persisted in regaling the court with gibes and enigmas. He deliberately made his riddles simple in order to flatter the king, who somehow still failed to respond to:

"**Your majesty, good sirs... the pocket of my motley is empty, and yet there is something in it! Do you know what it is?**"

HOP-FROG

Solution on page 213

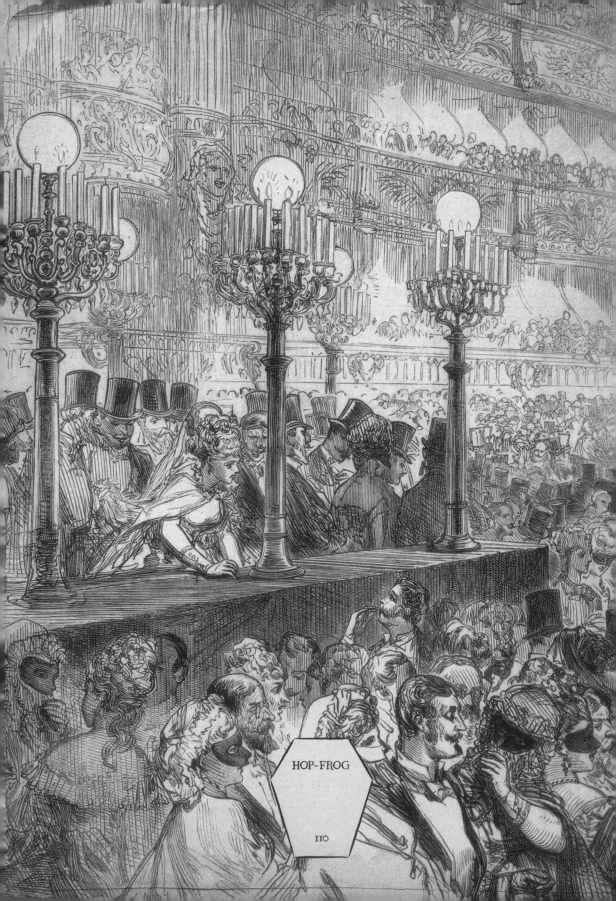

HOP-FROG

110

Setting A Lure

On some grand state occasion—I forget what—the king determined to have a masquerade. Whenever a masquerade, or any thing of that kind, occurred at our court, the talents of Hop-Frog were sure to be called into play. Hop-Frog was so inventive in the way of getting up pageants, suggesting novel characters, and arranging costume for **masked** balls that nothing could be done, it seems, without his assistance.

The night appointed for the fête had arrived. A gorgeous hall had been fitted up, with the whole court in a fever of expectation. Hop-Frog had included a **mystery** within each handwritten invitation:

"To attend the masquerade, please arrive at a time which if it were three hours later, it would be twice as long until midnight as it would be if it were four hours later".

What time did the masquerade start?

HOP-FROG

III

HOP-FROG

"Come here, Hop-Frog," said the king; "swallow this bumper to the health of your absent friends, and then let us have the benefit of your invention. We want characters for the masque—something novel, out of the way. We are wearied with this everlasting sameness. The wine will brighten your wits."

The monarch appeared to be in a very ill humour. He knew that Hop-Frog was not fond of wine, for it excited the poor cripple almost to madness and madness is no comfortable feeling. But the king loved his practical jokes and took pleasure in forcing Hop-Frog to drink and (as the king called it) "to be merry."

Hop-Frog endeavoured, as usual, to get up a jest in reply to these advances from the king but the effort was too much. It happened to be the poor fool's birthday, and the command to drink to his "absent friends" forced tears to his eyes. Many large, bitter drops fell into the goblet as he took it, humbly, from the hand of the tyrant.

"Ah! ha! ha! ha!" roared the latter, as Hop-Frog reluctantly drained the beaker. "See what a glass of good wine can do! Why, your eyes are shining already!"

Poor fellow! his large eyes gleamed, rather than shone.

"Come, Hop-Frog, lend us your assistance. Characters, we stand in need of characters—all of us—ha! ha! ha! Have you nothing to suggest?"

"Oh, I have something to suggest," said Hop-Frog, "But, first, a riddle—

How do you spell 'blind pig' in two letters?"

HOP-FROG

113

Solution on page 213

"I will equip you as ourang-outangs", proceeded the dwarf Hop-Frog, "leave all that to me. The resemblance shall be so striking, that the company of masqueraders will take you for real **beasts**—and of course, they will be as much terrified as astonished."

"Capital!" roared in chorus the monarch and his ministry.

Hop-Frog's mode of equipping the party as ourang-outangs was very simple, but effective enough for his purposes. The king and his ministers were first encased in tight-fitting stockinet shirts and drawers. They were then saturated with tar, which was then given a thick coating of flax. A long chain was passed about the waist of the king, and tied about all other members of the group. The five ourang-outangs, taking Hop-Frog's advice, waited patiently until midnight before making their appearance. The alarm among the masqueraders was prodigious, and filled the heart of the king with glee. They recovered, in some measure, and, beginning to regard the whole matter as a well-contrived pleasantry, set up a loud shout of laughter at the predicament of the apes.

"Leave them to me!" screamed Hop-Frog, his shrill voice making itself easily heard through the din. "I fancy I know know them, if I can only get a good look at them." Seizing a flambeau he leapt upon the king's head, holding down the torch to examine the ourang-outangs.

"Ah, ha! I begin to see who these people are, now!" Pretending to scrutinise the king more closely, he held the flambeau to the flaxen coat which instantly burst into a sheet of vivid flame. Soon the whole eight **ourang-outangs** were blazing fiercely, amid the shrieks of the multitude who gazed at them, horror-stricken, and without the power to render the slightest assistance.

"I now see **distinctly** what manner of people these maskers are. They are a great king and his seven privy councillors. As for myself, I am simply Hop-Frog, the jester—**and this is my last jest**".

Owing to the high combustibility of both the flax and the tar, he had scarcely made an end of his brief speech before the work of vengeance was complete. After three minutes the eight corpses swung in their chains, a **fetid**, blackened, hideous, and **indistinguishable** mass. If he'd had the dexterity for a larger flambeau he could have had his vengeance in only two minutes, but it mattered not. The cripple hurled his torch at them, clambered leisurely to the ceiling, and disappeared through the sky-light.

HOP-FROG

If Hop-Frog had used both sizes of the torch at the same time, how long would it have taken him to have killed the eight men?

HOP-FROG

115

Solution on page 213

THE FALL OF THE HOUSE OF USHER

During the whole of a dull, dark, and soundless day in the autumn of the year, when the clouds hung oppressively low in the heavens, I had been passing alone, on horseback, through a singularly dreary tract of country; and at length found myself, as the shades of the evening drew on, within view of the melancholy House of Usher.

I know not how it was—but, with the first glimpse of the building, a sense of insufferable gloom pervaded my spirit. I looked upon the scene before me—upon the mere house, and the simple landscape features of the domain—upon the bleak walls—upon the vacant eye-like windows—upon a few rank sedges—and upon a few white trunks of decayed trees—with an utter depression of soul which I can compare to no earthly sensation. There was an iciness, a sinking, a sickening of the heart—an unredeemed dreariness of thought which no goading of the imagination could torture into aught of the sublime. What was it—I paused to think—what was it that so unnerved me in the contemplation of the House of Usher? I attempted to distract myself with a whimsical old enigma—why is a plum-pudding like the ocean?—but, of course, it failed to cheer me as I already knew the answer.

Why is a plum-pudding like the ocean?

THE FALL
OF THE
HOUSE OF
USHER

119

Solution on page 214

In this mansion of gloom I now proposed to myself a sojourn of some weeks. Its proprietor, Roderick Usher, had been one of my boon companions in boyhood; but many years had elapsed since our last meeting. A letter, however, had lately reached me in a distant part of the country which, in its wildly importunate nature, had admitted of no other than a personal reply. The message gave evidence of nervous agitation. The writer spoke of acute bodily illness—of a mental disorder which oppressed him—and of an earnest desire to see me, as his best, and indeed his only, personal friend, with a view of attempting, by the cheerfulness of my society, some alleviation of his **malady**.

It was the manner in which all this, and much more, was said—it was the apparent heart that went with his request— which allowed me no room for hesitation; and I accordingly obeyed forthwith what I still considered a very singular summons.

Indeed, much of the letter made almost no sense at all, and this concerned me. What to make, for instance, of the passage where Usher observed:

"Some shrabs are clems. All clems are gwareks. Some gwareks are losas. Some losas are clems. Therefore, some shrabs are definitely losas. My dear friend, please help me—

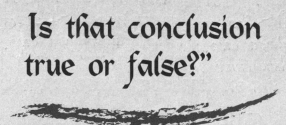

Is that conclusion true or false?"

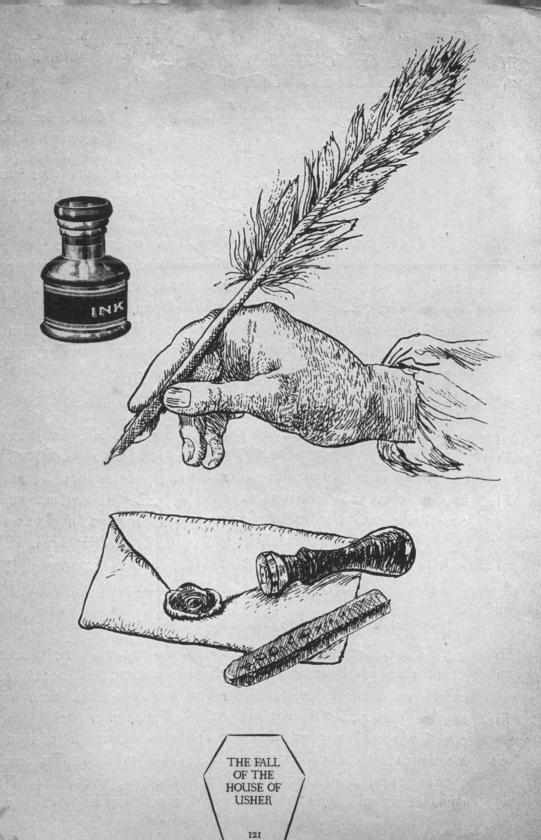

THE FALL
OF THE
HOUSE OF
USHER

121

Solution on page 214

An Atmosphere Peculiar

There can be no doubt that the consciousness of the rapid increase of my superstition—for why should I not so term it?—served mainly to accelerate the increase itself. It might have been for this reason, that, when I again uplifted my eyes to the house, there grew in my mind a strange fancy—a fancy so ridiculous, indeed, that I but mention it to show the vivid force of the sensations which oppressed me.

I had so worked upon my imagination as really to believe that about the whole mansion and domain there hung an atmosphere peculiar to themselves and their immediate vicinity—an atmosphere which had no affinity with the air of heaven, but which had reeked up from the decayed trees, and the grey wall, and the silent tarn—a pestilent and mystic vapour, dull, sluggish, faintly discernible, and leaden-hued.

Shaking off from my spirit what must have been a dream, I scanned more narrowly the real aspect of the building. Its principal feature was an excessive antiquity, yet all this was apart from any extraordinary dilapidation. No portion of the masonry had fallen; and there appeared to be a wild inconsistency between its still perfect adaptation of parts, and the crumbling condition of the individual stones. Beyond the extensive decay, however, the fabric gave little token of instability.

Perhaps the eye of a scrutinising observer might have discovered a barely perceptible fissure, which, extending from the roof of the building in front, made its way down the wall in a zigzag direction, until it became lost in the sullen waters of the tarn. Similarly, the two halves of the roof were at an unequal pitch. The left half, I would have ventured, sloped downwards at an angle of 60° while the right half boasted an angle of 70°. With a hope to stave off the gloom of the afternoon, I wondered to myself—

Suppose a rooster lays an egg directly on the peak, on which side of the roof would the egg fall?

THE FALL
OF THE
HOUSE OF
USHER

123

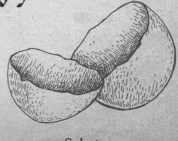

Solution on page 214

The Dimensions of Madness

Upon my entrance, Usher arose from a sofa on which he had been lying at full length, and greeted me with a **vivacious** warmth which had much in it, I at first thought, of an overdone cordiality. We sat down, and for some moments, while he spoke not, I gazed upon him with a feeling half of pity, half of awe. Surely, man had never before so terribly altered, in so brief a period, as had Roderick Usher!

A cadaverousness of complexion; in the exaggeration of the prevailing character of these features lay so much of change that I doubted the wan being to whom I spoke was the companion of my boyhood. The now ghastly pallor, the now miraculous lustre of the eye, above all things startled and even awed me. He spoke of his earnest desire to see me, and of the solace he expected me to afford him, before entering, at some length, into what he conceived to be the nature of his malady.

It was, he said, a constitutional and a family evil, and one for which he despaired to find a remedy. It displayed itself in a host of unnatural sensations. He suffered much from a morbid acuteness of the senses; the most insipid food was alone endurable; he could wear only garments of certain texture; the odours of all flowers were oppressive. To an anomalous species of terror I found him a bounden slave. "I shall perish," said he, "I must perish in this deplorable folly. I dread the events of the future, not in themselves, but in their results. I feel that the period will sooner or later arrive when I must abandon life and reason altogether."

I learned, at intervals, another singular feature of his mental condition. He was enchained by certain superstitious impressions in regard to the dwelling which he tenanted. He had become convinced, he explained, that the rooms had all changed in size at some point, but why this was he could not say. He thus spent much of his time marching from room to room with a measuring rod in hand, desperate to ensure that the dimensions were not shifting. The very room we were standing in, he told me, had a floor area of 24 feet by 48 feet, while its space diagonal was 56 feet. He had been about to measure the room's height when he spied my horse. I told him I already knew the answer, and he fixed his eyes—liquid, and luminous beyond comparison—upon me. "How tall is the room?" he beseeched, "I must understand."

THE FALL
OF THE
HOUSE OF
USHER

"How tall is the room?"

THE FALL
OF THE
HOUSE OF
USHER

125

Solution on page 214

It pained me to see Usher in such despair, that I did cast about for any earnest endeavour that might alleviate his melancholy. I suggested that we paint or read together, yet I could see the futility of all attempt at cheering a mind from which darkness poured forth upon all objects of the moral and physical universe, in one unceasing radiation of gloom.

The only occasion that day when I did succeed in rousing his attention, albeit fleetingly, was when I posed a problem to him of the nature that had consoled me upon my fateful arrival. I pointed out that there were more inhabitants of the nearest town than there were hairs on the head of any inhabitant within its districts, and that no one person was totally bald.

Did it follow then, I asked, that there must be at least two inhabitants with exactly the same number of hairs?

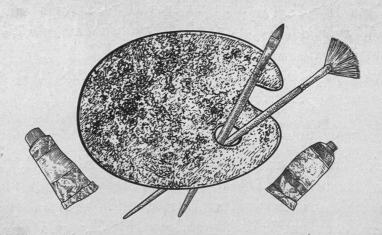

Solution on page 214

Usher admitted, although with hesitation, that much of the peculiar **gloom** which afflicted him could be traced to a more natural and palpable origin—to the severe and long-continued illness—indeed to the evidently approaching dissolution—of a tenderly beloved sister—his sole companion for long years—his last and only relative on earth. "Her decease," he said, with a bitterness which I can never forget, "has left me the last of the ancient race of the Ushers."

While he spoke, the lady Madeline (for so was she called) passed slowly through a remote portion of the apartment, and, without having noticed my presence, disappeared. I regarded her with an utter astonishment not unmingled with **dread**—and yet I found it impossible to account for such feelings. A sensation of stupor oppressed me, as my eyes followed her retreating steps. When a door, at length, closed upon her, my glance sought instinctively and eagerly the countenance of the brother—but he had buried his face in his hands.

The disease of the lady Madeline had long baffled the skill of her physicians. A settled apathy, a gradual wasting away of the person, and a confounding transformation of her speech were the unusual diagnosis. Usher told me how he'd come to understand that, in Madeline's mangled vocabulary, jire holver ool meant "torn fraying robes," plu queg holver meant "mend fraying heart" and kleest plu jire meant "mend robes often."

"I can hardly comprehend it," he said, apparently deaf to the similarly disfigured language in his own epistle to me—

"I have a 'torn heart'. How would you say that?"

THE FALL
OF THE
HOUSE OF
USHER

Solution on page 214

The Terrors he had Anticipated

"Not hear it?—I hear it, and **have** heard it. Many days have I heard it—oh, pity me, miserable wretch that I am!—yet I **dared** not speak! I have put her living in the tomb! Said I not that my senses were acute? I now tell you that I heard her first feeble movements in the hollow coffin, the grating of the iron hinges of her prison and her struggles within the coppered archway of the vault! Have I not heard her footstep on the stair? Do I not distinguish that heavy and horrible beating of her heart?" Here he sprang furiously to his feet, and shrieked out his syllables, as if in the effort were giving up his soul—"**I tell you that she now stands without the door!**"

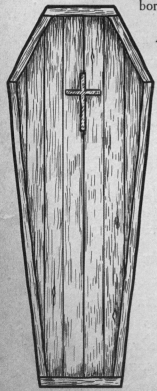

As if in the superhuman energy of his utterance there had been found the potency of a spell—without those doors did stand the lofty and enshrouded figure of Madeline. There was blood upon her white robes, and evidence of some bitter struggle upon every portion of her emaciated frame. With a low moaning cry, she fell heavily inward upon the person of her brother, and in her violent and now final death-agonies, bore him to the floor a corpse.

From that chamber, and from that mansion, I fled aghast. As I crossed the old causeway, I looked back: the radiance was that of the setting blood-red moon which now shone vividly through that once barely-discernible fissure that extended from the roof of the building to the base. While I gazed, this fissure rapidly widened—my brain reeled

THE FALL
OF THE
HOUSE OF
USHER

Solution on page 215

as I saw the mighty walls rushing asunder—there was a long tumultuous shouting sound like the voice of a thousand waters—and the deep and dank tarn at my feet closed sullenly and silently over the fragments of the "House of Usher".

A curious memory arose, unbidden, from that first night: "Why is the letter F like death?" Roderick had asked me, and I supposed that I would have some wait before I heard the answer.

"Why is the letter F like death?"

Edgar Allan Poe wrote this riddle-poem for someone in his life who had shown him "repeated kindness".

"Seldom we find," says Solomon Don Dunce,
"Half an idea in the profoundest sonnet.
Through all the flimsy things we see at once
As easily as through a Naples bonnet—
Trash of all trash!—how can a lady don it?
Yet heavier far than your Petrarchan stuff—
Owl-downy nonsense that the faintest puff
Twirls into trunk-paper the while you con it."
And, veritably, Sol is right enough.
The general tuckermanities are arrant
Bubbles—ephemeral and so transparent—
But this is, now,—you may depend upon it—
Stable, opaque, immortal—all by dint
Of the dear names that lie concealed within't.

Can you find their name hidden?

SONNET

SONNET

133

Solution on page 215

Of my country and of my family I have little to say. Ill usage and length of years have driven me from the one, and estranged me from the other. Hereditary wealth afforded me an education of no common order, and a contemplative turn of mind enabled me to methodise the stores which early study diligently garnered up. My deficiency of imagination has often been imputed as a crime; and the scepticism of my opinions has rendered me notorious. Upon the whole, no person could be less liable to be led away by the impractical schemes of superstition. I have thought proper to premise thus much, lest the incredible tale I have to tell should be considered the raving of a crude imagination, rather than the experience of a mind to which the **reveries** of fancy have been a dead letter and a nullity.

After many years spent in foreign travel, I sailed from the port of Batavia on an voyage to the Archipelago of the Sunda islands. I went as passenger—having no other inducement than a kind of nervous restlessness which haunted me. Our vessel was a beautiful ship of about four hundred tons of Malabar teak, copper-fastened and built in Bombay. She was freighted with cotton-wool and oil from the Lachadive islands, and also boasted coir, jaggeree, ghee, cocoa-nuts and a few cases of opium.

The stowage was clumsily done and the vessel consequently crank. Of the hundred **souls** on board, 65 had experience of working for the Dutch East India Company, 78 had worked for the John Company, and—most disconcertingly—13 had never sailed before. Before we set sail it would have been astute to question how many of the crew had experience of working for both companies, but we had left astuteness somewhere in Batavia.

How many of the crew had experience of working for both companies?

MS.
FOUND IN
A BOTTLE

134

Solution on page 215

Under the Weather

We got under way with a mere breath of wind, and proceeded along the eastern coast of Java without any incident to beguile the **monotony** of our course. One evening, leaning over the taffrail, I observed a very singular, isolated cloud, remarkable for its colour as for being the first we had seen since departure. I watched attentively until sunset, when it spread all at once to the eastward and westward. My notice was attracted by the dusky-red moon, and the peculiar character of the sea.

The latter was undergoing a rapid change, the water seeming more than usually transparent. The air became intolerably hot, loaded with spiral exhalations similar to those arising from heated iron. As night came on, all wind died away, and a more entire calm it is impossible to conceive. However, as the captain said he could perceive no indication of danger, he ordered the sails to be furled, and the anchor let go. No watch was set, and the crew stretched themselves upon the weather deck. I told the captain my fears; but he paid no attention to what I said. I went below— not without a full presentiment of evil. Indeed, every appearance warranted me in apprehending a Simoom.

My uneasiness prevented me from sleeping so I took to an exercise I had lately contrived to lull me by merit of its tedium and precision. This enterprise was to fill a sack with cotton-wool, doubling the quantity of cotton-wool every minute. It usually took me two hours to accomplish the feat, but my nerves were so jagged that I abandoned my task with the sack half-filled, and left my berth.

MS.
FOUND IN
A BOTTLE

136

Solution on page 216

I wasn't sure how long I had been below deck, but as I placed my foot upon the upper step of the companion-ladder, I was startled by a loud humming noise, like that of a mill-wheel, and before I could ascertain its meaning, I found the ship quivering. In the next instant, a **wilderness** of foam hurled us upon our beam-ends, and rushing over us fore and aft, swept the entire decks from stem to stern. The extreme fury of the blast proved, in a great measure, the salvation of the ship. Although completely water-logged, yet, as her masts had gone by the board, she rose, after a minute, heavily from the sea, and staggering awhile beneath the immense pressure of the tempest, finally righted.

How long had I been below deck?

A Stripped Deck

By what miracle I escaped destruction, it is impossible to say; the whirlpool of mountainous and foaming ocean within which we were engulfed were beyond the wildest imagination. With great difficulty I gained my feet, and after a while heard the voice of an old Swede, who had shipped with us at the moment of our leaving port. We soon discovered that we were the sole survivors of the accident. All on deck, with the exception of ourselves, had been swept overboard—the captain and mates must have perished as they slept, for the cabins were deluged with water.

Without assistance, we could expect to do little for the security of the ship. We scudded with frightful velocity before the sea, and the water made clear breaches over us. The frame-work of our stem was shattered excessively, and, in almost every respect, we had received considerable injury.

For five entire days and nights—during which our only subsistence was a small quantity of jaggeree, procured with great difficulty from the forecastle—the hulk flew at a rate defying computation, before rapidly succeeding flaws of wind, which, without equalling the first **violence** of the Simoom, were still more terrific than any tempest I had before encountered.

During this period we had little to do except play cards with the Swede's sodden, warped deck, and apprehend the numerous ways in which we would likely expire. An imaginary ham was played for during each game, with the hams not counted until the end of the week. We decided—or it is altogether more accurate to state that the old Swede decided—that if at any time we had the same number of wins, the hams would be cancelled. At the end of the five days I had won four matches and possessed no hams, imaginary or otherwise, and the Swede had won three hams. We tried to calculate how many rounds of cards had been played, but it was impossible to keep track in the dizzying tumult.

How many rounds of cards had been played?

MS.
FOUND IN
A BOTTLE

138

Solution on page 216

Calm Seas, Prosperous Voyage

We waited in vain for the arrival of the sixth day—that day, for the
Swede never did arrive. Enshrouded in pitchy darkness, we could not
have seen an object at twenty paces. Eternal night continued to envelop
us, unrelieved by the phosphoric sea-brilliancy to which we had been
accustomed in the tropics.

All around was horror, and thick gloom, and a black **sweltering** desert.
Superstitious terror crept by degrees into the spirit of the old Swede, and
my own soul was wrapped up in silent wonder. We neglected all care of
the ship, securing ourselves to the stump of the mizzen-mast and looking
out bitterly into the world of ocean. We had no means of calculating
time, nor could we form any guess of our situation. We were, however,
well aware of having made farther south than any previous navigators, and
felt great amazement at not meeting with the usual impediments of ice.

In the meantime every moment threatened to be our last—every
mountainous billow hurried to overwhelm us. That we were not
instantly buried by the swell is a miracle. My companion reminded me
of the excellent qualities of our ship; but I could not help feeling utter
hopelessness, and prepared myself for that death which I thought nothing

Solution on page 216

could defer beyond an hour. The Swede, for his part, attempted
to bring light to our mood with stories of his boyhood, but these were
often rendered unintelligible by frequent lapses into his native tongue.

The Swede's tales grew taller as the sea grew more appalling.
His father, he swore, had decided to **bequeath** his estate to whichever of
his two sons proved most deserving. They would sail around the nation's
coastline and the son whose skiff finished last would inherit everything.
The sons spent weeks miserably inching along before they docked at an
inn to discuss the matter. After finishing their drinks they leapt into
the boats and sailed as fast as they could.

What did the sons decide to do? Regrettably I cannot
tell you, for that part of the story was told in Swedish.

What did the sons decide to do?

MS.
FOUND IN
A BOTTLE.

141

A scream from my companion broke fearfully upon the night. "Almighty God!" cried he, shrieking in my ears, "See! See!"

Casting my eyes upwards, I beheld a spectacle which froze the current of my blood. Upon the summit of a wave directly above us hovered a gigantic ship of perhaps four thousand tons. Her huge hull was of a deep dingy black, unrelieved by any of the customary carvings of a ship. A single row of brass cannon protruded from her open ports, and dashed from their polished surfaces the fires of innumerable battle-lanterns, which swung to and fro about her rigging.

When we first discovered her, her bows were alone to be seen, as she rose slowly from the dim and horrible gulf beyond her. For a moment of intense **terror** she paused upon the giddy pinnacle, as if in contemplation of her own sublimity, then trembled and tottered, and—came down. I know not what self-possession came over my spirit. Staggering as far aft as I could, I awaited fearlessly the ruin that was to overwhelm.

Our own vessel was at length ceasing from her struggles, and sinking with her head to the sea. The shock of the descending mass struck her, consequently, in that portion of her frame which was already under water, and the inevitable result was to hurl me, with irresistible violence, upon the rigging of the stranger. This must be some manner of illusion, I thought—a ruse borne by the ship herself. But then, as the moth-eaten naval enigma went—

When does a ship tell a falsehood?

MS.
FOUND IN
A BOTTLE

Solution on page 216

Like Ghosts Of Buried Centuries

It is long since I first trod the deck of this terrible ship, and the rays of my destiny are gathering to a focus. Incomprehensible men! Wrapped up in meditations of a kind which I cannot divine, they pass me by unnoticed. Concealment is folly on my part, for the people will not see. It was no long while ago that I ventured into the captain's private cabin and took the materials with which I write. I may not find an opportunity of transmitting it to the world, but I will not fail to make the endeavour. At the last moment I will enclose the MS. in a bottle, and cast it within the sea.

About an hour ago, I made bold to thrust myself among a group of the crew. They paid me no manner of attention, and, although I stood in the very midst of them all, seemed utterly unconscious of my presence. They all bore about them the marks of a hoary old age. Their knees trembled with infirmity; their shoulders were bent double with decrepitude; their shrivelled skins rattled in the wind. Around them, on every part of the deck, lay scattered mathematical instruments of the most quaint and obsolete construction. The crew mutter to themselves in some low peevish syllables of a foreign tongue, and even when the speaker is close at my elbow, their voice seems to reach from the distance of a mile. I understand almost nothing; I know that "glup pollok" means cyclone approaching, "glup terook congra" means immense approaching Simoom and "terook kelv" means immense typhoon, but even then I cannot even decipher which word means Simoom.

The ship has continued her terrific course due south, and rolling every moment her top-gallant yardarms into the most appalling hell of water which it can enter into the mind of man to imagine. A curiosity to penetrate the mysteries of these awful regions predominates even over my despair, and will reconcile me to the most hideous aspect of death. It is evident that we are hurrying onwards to some exciting knowledge—some never-to-be imparted secret, whose attainment is destruction.

MS.
FOUND IN
A BOTTLE

144

Solution on page 216

Oh, horror upon horror! the ice opens suddenly to the right, and to the left, and we are whirling dizzily, in immense concentric circles. Little time will be left me to ponder upon my destiny—the circles rapidly grow small—we are plunging madly within the grasp of the whirlpool—and amid a roaring, and bellowing, and thundering of ocean and of tempest, the ship is quivering, oh God! and—going down.

Which word means Simoom?

THE
TELL-TALE
HEART

True!—nervous—very, very dreadfully nervous I had been and am; but why will you say that I am mad? The disease had sharpened my senses—not destroyed—not dulled them. Above all was the sense of hearing acute. I heard all things in the heaven and in the earth. I heard many things in hell. How, then, am I mad? Hearken! and observe how healthily—how calmly I tell you the whole story.

It is impossible to say how first the idea entered my brain; but once conceived, it haunted me day and night. Object there was none. Passion there was none. I loved the old man. He had never wronged me. He had never given me insult. For his gold I had no desire. In our many years of knowing each other, he had only even caused me frustration once, when he embarrassed me with a riddle—

"Does any word contain all the vowels?"

THE
TELL-TALE
HEART

148

Solution on page 217

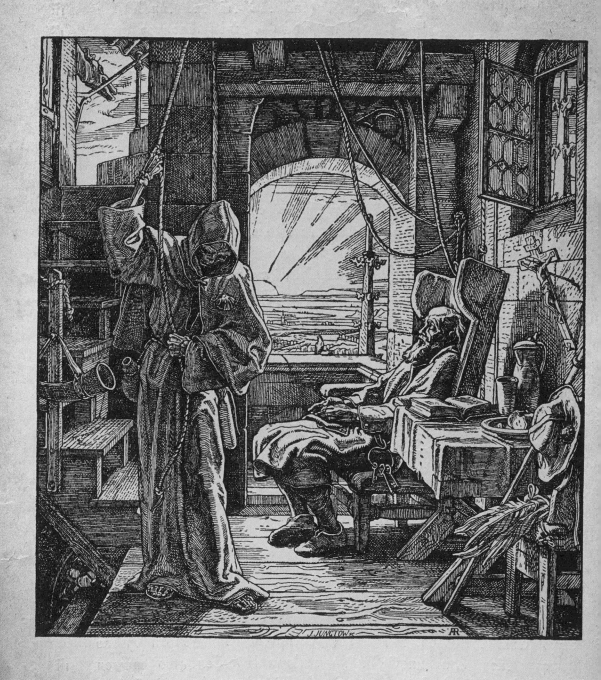

THE
TELL-TALE
HEART

150

I think it was his eye! yes, it was this! One of his eyes resembled that of a **vulture**—a pale blue eye, with a film over it. Whenever it fell upon me, my blood ran cold; and so by degrees—very gradually—I made up my mind to take the life of the old man, and thus rid myself of the eye for ever.

Now this is the point. You fancy me mad. Madmen know nothing. But you should have seen me. You should have seen how wisely I proceeded—with what caution—with what foresight—with what dissimulation I went to work! I was never kinder to the old man than during the whole week before I killed him. I even responded in good humour to his riddles, hatching ones of my own. He suspected nothing when I remarked—

"Iron roof, glass walls, burns and burns and never falls. What am I?"

THE
TELL-TALE
HEART

Solution on page 217

Sleeping Dogs

Every night, an hour or two before midnight, I turned the latch of his door and opened it—oh, so gently! And then, when I had made an opening sufficient for my head, I put in a dark lantern, all closed so that no light shone out, and then I thrust in my head. Oh, you would have laughed to see how **cunningly** I thrust it in! I moved it slowly—very, very slowly, so that I might not disturb the old man's sleep.

It took me an hour to place my whole head within the opening so far that I could see him as he lay upon his bed, a Cur curled up at his feet. Ha!—would a madman have been so wise as this? And then, when my head was well in the room, I undid the lantern cautiously—oh, so cautiously—cautiously (for the hinges creaked)—I undid it just so much that a single thin ray fell upon the vulture eye. And this I did for seven long nights, but I found the eye always closed; and so it was impossible to do the work; for it was not the old man who vexed me, but his Evil Eye.

The hardest part of this **endeavour** was avoiding the attention of the old man's dogs. Like their master, they would usually be sleeping at this hour, but as I didn't want to take anything for granted—as cunning as I was—I would check in on them before I began my routine. The problem was that I could never

THE
TELL-TALE
HEART

152

quite tally how many he had. I knew that all of the dogs were Plott Hounds except three, all of the dogs were Blue Lacys except three, and he also had a Mountain Feist.

For seven long nights, I stared upon that closed vulture eye, and tried to work out—

How many dogs did the old man own?

THE
TELL-TALE
HEART

153

Solution on page 217

I had my head in, and was about to open the lantern, when my thumb slipped upon the tin fastening, and the old man sprang up in the bed, crying out—"Who's there?" I kept quite still and said nothing. For a whole hour I did not move a muscle, and in the meantime I did not hear him lie down. He was still sitting up in the bed listening;—just as I have done, night after night, hearkening to the death watches in the wall.

Presently I heard a slight groan, and I knew it was the groan of mortal terror. It was not pain or grief—oh, no!—it was the low stifled sound that arises from the bottom of the soul when overcharged with awe. I knew the sound well. Many a night, when all the world slept, it has welled up from my own bosom, deepening, with its dreadful echo, the terrors that distracted me.

I knew what the old man felt, and pitied him, although I chuckled at heart. I knew that he had been lying awake ever since the first slight noise, when he had turned in the bed. His fears had been ever since growing upon him. He had been trying to fancy them causeless, but could not. He had been saying to himself—"It is nothing but the wind in the chimney—it is only a mouse crossing the floor," or "it is merely a cricket which has made a single chirp."

Yes, he has been trying to comfort himself with these suppositions; but he had found all in vain. **All in vain;** because Death, in approaching him, had stalked with his black shadow before him, and enveloped the victim. And it was the mournful influence of the unperceived shadow that caused him to feel—although he neither saw nor heard—to feel the presence of my head within the room.

I know not how long I spent leaning into that bedchamber. It seemed as if I had never been anywhere else, but I understood how that could not be the case. I shifted my gaze to the clock by the old man's bed, waiting for my moment. I had pictured my triumph over and over again: at midnight I would open my lantern precisely as I heard the clock's final gong.

Surely, it would not be long now, for that evening it had only taken seven seconds for the clock to strike seven gongs. How long would it take to hear all twelve, I wondered, as a soft ticking came from the bed.

What time was it?

THE
TELL-TALE
HEART

155

Solution on page 217

The Beginning of the End

When I had waited a long time, very patiently, without hearing him lie down, I resolved to open a very, very little crevice in the lantern. So I opened it until, at length, a single dim ray, like the thread of the spider, shot from out the crevice and full upon the vulture eye. It was open-wide, wide open—and I grew furious as I gazed upon it. I saw it with perfect **distinctness**—all a dull blue, with a hideous veil over it that chilled the marrow in my bones; but I could see nothing else of the old man's face or person: for I had directed the ray as if by instinct, precisely upon the damned spot.

What you mistake for madness is but over-acuteness of the senses—now, I say, there came to my ears a low, dull, quick sound, such as a watch makes when enveloped in cotton. I knew that sound well too. It was the beating of the old man's heart. It increased my fury, as the beating of a drum stimulates the soldier into courage. But even yet I refrained and kept still. I scarcely breathed. Meantime the hellish tattoo of the heart increased. It grew quicker and quicker, and louder and louder every instant. The old man's terror must have been extreme! And now at the dead hour of the night, amid the dreadful silence of that old house, so strange a noise as this excited me to uncontrollable terror. Yet, for some minutes longer I refrained and stood still. But the beating grew louder, louder! I thought the heart must

THE
TELL-TALE
HEART

burst. And now a new **anxiety** seized me—the sound would be heard by a neighbour! The old man's hour had come! With a loud yell, I threw open the lantern and leaped into the room.

He shrieked once—once only. In an instant I dragged him to the floor, and pulled the heavy bed over him.

"Here's one last riddle for you," I whispered, "I am the beginning of the end, and the end of time and space. I am essential to creation, and I surround every place. What am I?" I then smiled gaily, to find the deed so far done. But, for many minutes, the heart beat on with a muffled sound. This, however, did not vex me; it would not be heard through the wall. At length it ceased. His eye would trouble me no more. The old man was dead.

"I am the beginning of the end,
and the end of time and space.
I am essential to creation,
and I surround every place.
What am I?"

THE
TELL-TALE
HEART

157

Solution on page 217

The Burying of his Hideous Heart!

If still you think me mad, you will think so no longer when I describe the wise precautions I took for the concealment of the body. The night waned, and I worked hastily, but in silence. First of all I **dismembered** the corpse. I cut off the head and the arms and the legs. I then took up three planks from the flooring of the chamber, and deposited all between the scantlings.

I then replaced the boards so cleverly, so cunningly, that no human eye—not even his—could have detected any thing wrong. There was nothing to wash out—no stain of any kind—no blood-spot whatever. I had been too wary for that. A tub had caught all!

When I had made an end of these labours, it was four o'clock— still dark as midnight. It had been a perfect triumph, yet I couldn't help but reflect on how he might have done it, if such a thing were possible. I concealed the body of the old man, every single bit of him, in two hours, but I bet if he had **disposed** of himself—ha! Ha!—it would have taken him three.

When would I have finished if we had done the job side by side, I pondered, as there came a knocking at the street door.

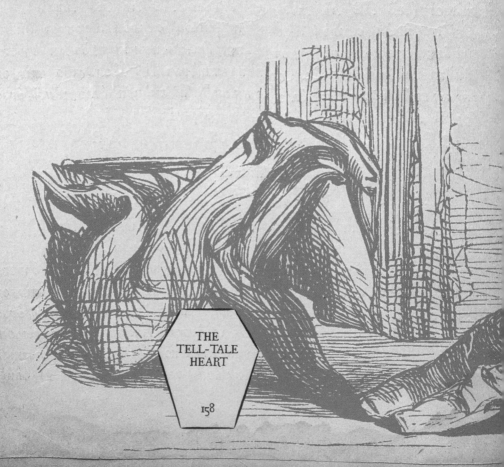

THE
TELL-TALE
HEART

158

When would I have finished if we had done the job side by side?

Solution on page 217

A Low, Dull, Quick Sound

I opened the door with a light heart, for what had I now to fear?

There entered three men, who introduced themselves, with perfect suavity, as officers of the police. A shriek had been heard by a neighbour, suspicion of foul play had been aroused and the officers had been deputed to search the premises. The shriek, I said, was my own in a dream, and the old man was absent in the country. I took my visitors all over the house. I led them, at length, to his chamber. I showed them his treasures, secure, undisturbed. In the enthusiasm of my confidence, I brought chairs into the room, and suggested they rest from their fatigues, while I myself, in the wild audacity of my triumph, placed my own seat upon the very spot beneath which reposed the corpse of the victim.

The officers were satisfied. My manner had convinced them. They sat, and while I answered cheerily, they chatted familiar things. But, ere long, I felt myself getting pale and wished them gone. My head ached, and I fancied a ringing in my ears: but still they chatted. I talked more freely to get rid of the feeling: but it continued and gained definitiveness—until, at length, I found that the noise was not within my ears. No doubt I now grew very pale;—but I talked more vehemently, and with a heightened voice. Yet the sound increased—and what could I do? I gasped for breath—and yet the officers heard it not.

Why would they not be gone? I arose and paced the floor to and fro with heavy strides, as if excited to fury by the observation of the men—but the noise steadily increased. I tried to fool my senses with complicated thoughts, such as what would be the height of a pole made up of all the millimetre cubes in one cubic metre, if placed one on top of another?—but the noise steadily increased. Oh God! what could I do? I foamed—I raved—I swore! I swung the chair upon which I had been sitting, and grated it upon the boards, but the noise arose over all and continually increased. It grew louder—louder—louder! And still the men chatted pleasantly, and smiled. Was it possible they heard not? Almighty God!—no, no! They heard!—they suspected!—they knew!—they were making a mockery of my horror! Any thing was better than this agony! Any thing was more tolerable than this derision! I could bear those hypocritical smiles no longer! I felt that I must scream or die!—and now—again!—hark! louder! louder! louder! louder!

"Villains," I shrieked, "dissemble no more! I admit the deed!—tear up the planks!—here, here!—it is the beating of his hideous heart!"

THE
TELL-TALE
HEART

160

Solution on page 218

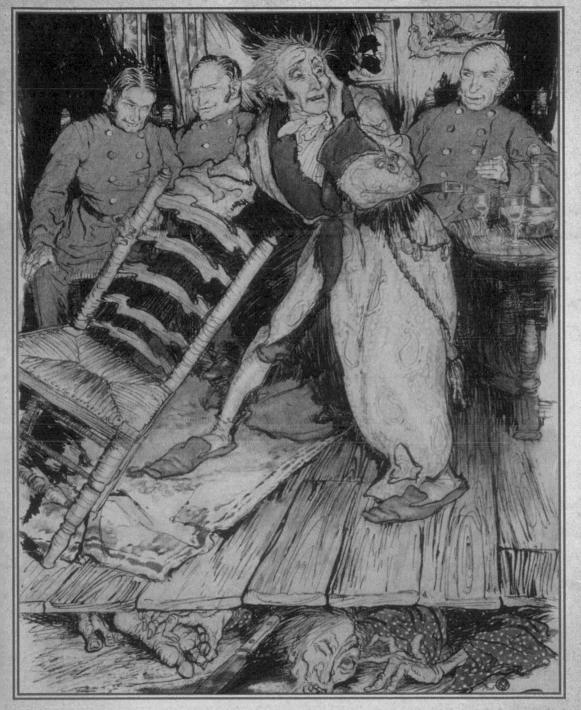

What would be the height of a pole made up of all the millimetre cubes in one cubic metre, if placed one on top of another?

Edgar Allan Poe wrote this riddle-poem in the keepsake album of his cousin, Ms. Herring.

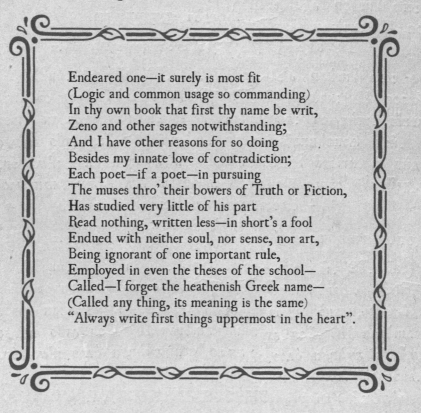

Endeared one—it surely is most fit
(Logic and common usage so commanding)
In thy own book that first thy name be writ,
Zeno and other sages notwithstanding;
And I have other reasons for so doing
Besides my innate love of contradiction;
Each poet—if a poet—in pursuing
The muses thro' their bowers of Truth or Fiction,
Has studied very little of his part
Read nothing, written less—in short's a fool
Endued with neither soul, nor sense, nor art,
Being ignorant of one important rule,
Employed in even the theses of the school—
Called—I forget the heathenish Greek name—
(Called any thing, its meaning is the same)
"Always write first things uppermost in the heart".

Can you find her name hidden within?

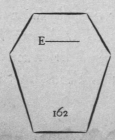

E———

162

163

Solution on page 218

MORELLA

164

With a feeling of deep yet most singular affection I regarded my friend Morella. Thrown by accident into her society many years ago, my soul, from our first meeting, burned with fires it had never before known; but the fires were not of Eros, and bitter and tormenting to my spirit was the gradual conviction that I could in no manner define their unusual meaning. Yet we met; and fate bound us together at the altar; and I never spoke of passion, nor thought of love.

Morella's erudition was profound. As I hope to live, her talents were of no common order—her powers of mind were gigantic. I felt this, and, in many matters, became her pupil. I soon, however, found that, perhaps on account of her education, she placed before me a number of the most complicated bewilderments. These were her favourite and constant study— and that, in process of time they became my own, should be attributed to the simple but effectual influence of habit and example. I had been lulled, falsely, into an impression of security by the first of such problems, when she strode up to me one morning and said:

"Could it be possible for there to be 53 Tuesdays in a non-leap year? What is the probability of such a thing?"

MORELLA

165

Solution on page 218

Like A Shadow Upon The Soul

The time had arrived when the mystery of my wife's manner oppressed me as a spell. I could no longer bear the touch of her wan fingers, nor the low tone of her musical language, nor the lustre of her melancholy eyes. And she knew all this, but did not upbraid. She seemed conscious of a cause, to me unknown, for the gradual alienation of my regard. And, indeed; in time, the crimson spot settled steadily upon the cheek, and the blue **veins** upon the pale forehead became prominent; and, one instant, my nature melted into pity, but, in the next, my soul sickened and became giddy as one who gazes down into some dreary and unfathomable abyss.

Shall I then say that I longed with a consuming desire for the moment of Morella's decease? I did; but the fragile spirit clung to its tenement of clay for many irksome months—until I grew furious through delay, and, with the heart of a fiend, cursed the days, and the hours, and the bitter moments, which seemed to lengthen as her gentle life declined— like shadows in the dying of the day.

But one autumnal evening, when the winds lay still in heaven, Morella called me to her bedside. There was a dim mist over all the earth, and a warm glow upon the waters, and, amid the rich October leaves of the forest, a rainbow from the firmament had surely fallen.

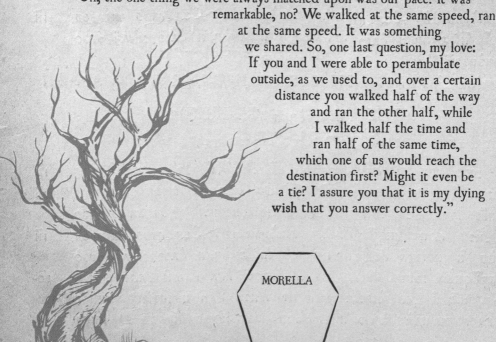

"It is a day of days," she said; "a day of all days either to live or die. Oh, the one thing we were always matched upon was our pace. It was remarkable, no? We walked at the same speed, ran at the same speed. It was something we shared. So, one last question, my love: If you and I were able to perambulate outside, as we used to, and over a certain distance you walked half of the way and ran the other half, while I walked half the time and ran half of the same time, which one of us would reach the destination first? Might it even be a tie? I assure you that it is my dying wish that you answer correctly."

MORELLA

Which one of us would reach the destination first?

MORELLA

167

Solution on page 218

MORELLA

168

I kissed her forehead, and she continued: "I am dying, yet shall I live. Within me is a pledge of that affection—ah, how little!—which you did not feel for me. And when my spirit departs shall the child live—your child and mine. But your days shall be days of sorrow, for the hours of your happiness are over; and joy is not gathered twice in a life."

"Morella!" I cried, " Morella! How do you know this?"—but she turned away her face upon the pillow, and, a slight tremor coming over her limbs, she thus died, and I heard her voice no more. Yet, as she had foretold, her child—to which in dying she had given birth, which breathed not until the mother breathed no more—a daughter, lived. And she grew strangely in stature and intellect, and was the perfect resemblance of her who had departed, and I loved her with a love more fervent than I had believed it possible to feel for any denizen of earth. Strange, indeed, was her rapid increase in bodily size—but terrible, oh! terrible were the tumultuous thoughts which crowded upon me while watching the development of her mental being!

As years rolled away, and I gazed, day after day, upon her holy, and mild, and eloquent face, and pored over her maturing form, day after day did I discover new points of resemblance in the child to her mother, the melancholy and the dead. She shared her mother's keen passion for quandaries, of which she knew intimately in spite of the rigorous seclusion of my home.

"Which letter of the alphabet can you add four letters to without changing its pronunciation?" she once asked, and I could have sworn that it was a question her mother had also posed to me. Hourly grew darker these shadows of similitude, and more full, and more definite, and more perplexing, and more hideously terrible in their aspect.

"Which letter of the alphabet can you add four letters to without changing its pronunciation?"

MORELLA

169

Solution on page 219

My daughter remained nameless upon the earth. "My child" and "my love" were the designations usually prompted by a father's affection, and the isolation of her days precluded all other intercourse. Morella's name died with her at her death. But at length the ceremony of baptism presented to my mind, in its unnerved and agitated condition, a present **deliverance** from the terrors of my destiny. And at the baptismal font I hesitated for a name.

What prompted me, then, to disturb the memory of the buried dead? What demon urged me to breathe that sound which was wont to make ebb the purple blood in torrents from the temples to the heart? What fiend spoke from the recesses of my soul, when, amid those dim aisles, and in the silence of the night, I whispered within the ears of the holy man the syllables—Morella? What more than fiend convulsed the features of my child, and overspread them with hues of death, as, starting at that scarcely audible sound, she turned her glassy eyes from the earth to heaven, and, falling prostrate on the black slabs of our ancestral vault, responded—"I am here! If 28 equals 24 and 68 equals 76, what does 48 equal?" A cruel, final jape!

Years—years may pass away, but the memory of that epoch—never! The winds of the firmament breathed but one sound within my ears, and the ripples upon the sea murmured evermore—Morella. But she died; and with my own hands I bore her to the tomb; and I laughed with a long and **bitter** laugh as I found no traces of the first, in the charnel where I laid the second, Morella.

"If 28 equals 24 and 68 equals 76, what does 48 equal?"

MORELLA

170

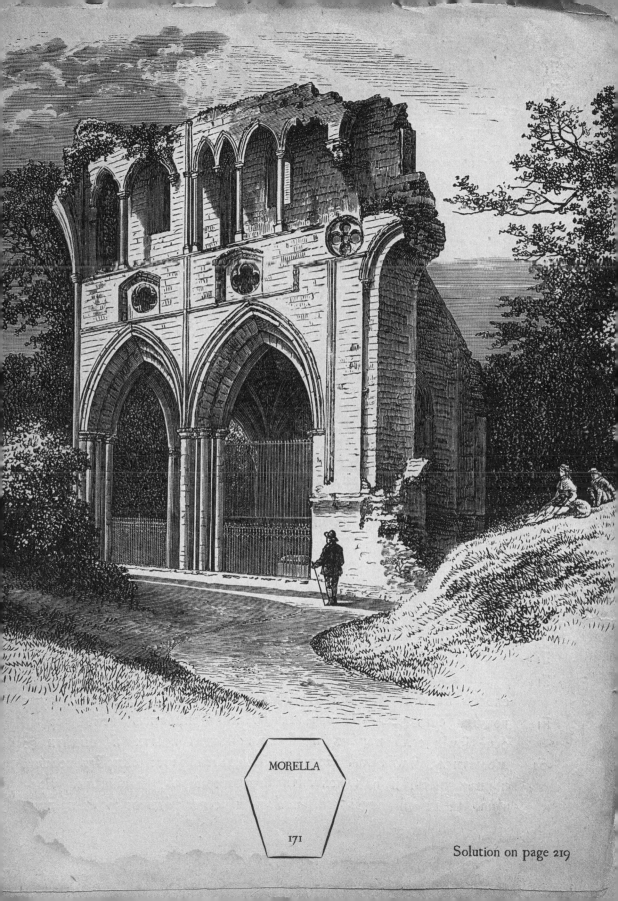

MORELLA

171

Solution on page 219

THE
BLACK CAT

For the most wild, yet most homely narrative which I am about to pen, I neither expect nor solicit belief. Mad indeed would I be to expect it, in a case where my very senses reject their own evidence. Yet, mad am I not—and very surely do I not dream. But to-morrow I die, and to-day I would unburden my soul. My immediate purpose is to place before the world, plainly, succinctly, and without comment, a series of mere household events. In their consequences, these events have terrified—have tortured—have destroyed me. Yet I will attempt to expound them.

From my infancy I was noted for the docility and humanity of my disposition. My tenderness of heart was even so conspicuous as to make me the jest of my companions. I was especially fond of animals, deriving from it one of my principal sources of pleasure, and was indulged by my parents with a great variety of pets. With these I spent most of my time, and never was so happy as when feeding and caressing them.

There is something in the unselfish and self-sacrificing love of a brute, which goes directly to the heart of him who has had occasion to test the paltry friendship and gossamer fidelity of mere Man. Indeed, my most treasured memory is a visit to a travelling menagerie containing such a spectrum of wonders that I could scarcely believe its existence. I remember—as vividly as if it had taken place this afternoon—pulling on the long, gilded sleeve of the showman in charge and asking him how many birds and beasts he owned.

"Dear child, that is my secret to keep," he said, "but I can tell you there are 45 heads and 150 feet!" For the entire homeward journey I beseeched my parents to tell me how many beasts and how many birds were in the menagerie, but was met with the silence to which I had become so accustomed.

How many beasts and birds were in the menagerie?

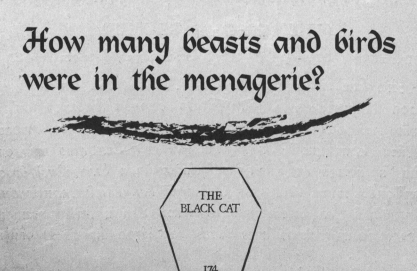

THE
BLACK CAT

174

Solution on page 219

A Bottle Uncorked

I married early, and was happy to find in my wife a disposition not uncongenial with my own. Observing my partiality for domestic pets, she lost no opportunity of procuring those of the most agreeable kind. We had birds, gold fish, a fine dog, rabbits, a small monkey and a **cat**. This latter was a remarkably large and beautiful animal, entirely black, and sagacious to an astonishing degree. In speaking of his intelligence, my wife, who at heart was not a little tinctured with superstition, made frequent allusion to the ancient popular notion, which regarded all black cats as **witches** in disguise— not that she was ever **serious** upon this point.

Pluto—this was the cat's name—was my favourite pet and playmate. I alone fed him, and he attended me wherever I went about the house. It was even with difficulty that I could prevent him from following me through the streets. Our friendship lasted, in this manner, for several years, during which my general temperament and character—through fiendish Intemperance— had experienced a radical alteration. I grew, day by day, more moody, irritable, regardless of others.

My pets, of course, were made to feel the change. I not only neglected, but ill-used them. For Pluto, however, I still retained sufficient regard to restrain me from maltreating him, as I made no scruple of maltreating the others when by accident, or through affection, they came in my way. But my disease grew upon me, and at length even Pluto began to experience the effects of my ill temper.

Solution on page 220

One night, much intoxicated, I was roundly humiliated at one of my haunts about town. A fellow drinker had asked, by way of a sally, what part of London is in France? All present had laughed cruelly when I answered incorrectly. Returning home, I fancied that the cat avoided my presence, as if in shame. I seized him; at which point, in his fright at my violence, he inflicted a slight wound upon my hand with his teeth. The **fury** of a demon instantly possessed me. I knew myself no longer. My original soul seemed, at once, to take its flight from my body; and a more than fiendish malevolence, gin-nurtured, thrilled every fibre of my frame. I took from my waistcoat-pocket a pen-knife, opened it, grasped the poor beast by the throat, and deliberately cut one of its eyes from the socket! I blush, I burn, I shudder, while I pen this damnable atrocity.

What part of
London is in France?

THE
BLACK CAT

177

Wrong for Wrong's Sake

When reason returned with the morning and I had slept off the fumes of the night's debauch, I experienced a sentiment half of horror, half of remorse; but it was, at best, a feeble and equivocal feeling, and the soul remained untouched. I again plunged into excess, and soon drowned in alcohol all memory of the deed.

In the meantime, the cat slowly recovered. The socket of the lost eye presented, it is true, a frightful appearance, but he no longer seemed to suffer any pain. He went about the house as usual, but, as might be expected, fled in extreme terror at my approach. I had so much of my old heart left, as to be at first grieved by this evident dislike on the part of a creature which had once so loved me. But this feeling soon gave place to irritation. I experienced an unfathomable longing of the soul to vex itself, to offer violence to its own nature and finally consummate the injury I had inflicted.

One morning, in cool blood, I slipped a noose about its neck and hung it to the limb of a tree;—hung it with tears streaming from my eyes, and with the bitterest remorse at my heart;—hung it because I knew that it had loved me, and because I felt it had given me no reason of offence;—hung it because I knew that in so doing I was committing a sin that would so jeopardize my immortal soul as to place it even beyond the infinite mercy of God.

On the night of the day on which the cruel deed was done, I fled to my nearest tavern and proceeded to imbibe until I was removed. All I remember is staring at my empty glass and being unable to recall what I had just drunk, then barking at the bartender: "If this was wine, I want rum, and if this was gin, bring me wine, but if this was rum, bring me gin!"

The bartender brought wine and told me what my previous drink had been, but no sooner had he said than it had left my mind. Later, I was aroused from sleep by the cry of fire. The curtains of my bed were in flames. The whole house was blazing. It was with great difficulty that my wife and myself made our escape. The destruction was complete. My worldly wealth was swallowed up, and I resigned myself thenceforward to despair.

THE
BLACK CAT

What had my previous drink been?

Solution on page 220

For months I could not rid myself of the phantasm of the cat; and there came back into my spirit a half-sentiment that seemed, but was not, remorse. I went so far as to regret the loss of the animal, and to look for another pet of the same species, and of somewhat similar appearance, with which to supply its place.

One night as I sat, half stupefied, in a den for more than infamy, my attention was drawn to some black object, reposing upon the head of one of the immense hogsheads of Rum which constituted the chief furniture of the apartment. It was a black cat, fully as large as Pluto, and closely resembling him in every respect but one. Pluto had not a white hair upon any portion of his body; but this cat had a large, indefinite splotch of white, covering nearly the whole breast. Upon my touching him, he immediately arose, purred loudly, rubbed against my hand, and appeared delighted with my notice. This, then, was the very creature of which I was in search. I at once offered to purchase it of the landlord; but he made no claim to it—knew nothing of it—had never seen it before. I continued my caresses, and, when I prepared to go home, the animal evinced a disposition to accompany me. I permitted it to do so; occasionally stooping and patting it as I proceeded. In my stupor, however, I was unable to recall where I lived.

I knew that I lived on a long street, and that on my side of the street the houses were numbered 1, 2, 3, and so on. My wife had told me once that all of the house numbers on one side of us added up to exactly the same as the house numbers on the other side. There were more than 50 houses on our side of the street, I was sure, and fewer than 500, but that constituted the outer reaches of my knowledge on the subject.

"Do you know what my house number is?" I asked the cat, but it just watched me, half-curious, half-something else.

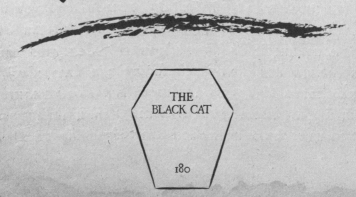

"Do you know what my house number is?"

THE
BLACK CAT

180

THE
BLACK CAT

181

Solution on page 220

I soon found a dislike to the cat arising within me. This was the reverse of what I had anticipated—its evident fondness for myself rather disgusted and annoyed. By slow degrees, these feelings rose into **bitterness**; I came to look upon it with unutterable loathing, and to flee silently from its presence. What added, no doubt, to my hatred, was the discovery, on the morning after I brought it home, that it also had been deprived of one of its eyes. This circumstance, however, only endeared it to my wife, who possessed that humanity of feeling which had once been my distinguishing trait.

With my aversion to this cat, however, its partiality for myself seemed to increase. It followed my footsteps with a pertinacity which it would be difficult to make the reader comprehend. Whenever I sat, it would crouch beneath my chair, or spring upon my knees, covering me with its loathsome caresses. Over a period of five days the cat left **thirty** dead mice on our doorstep, leaving three more each day than on the day before. My mind ached to even calculate how many mice were caught by the cat on the first day. At such times, although I longed to destroy it with a blow, I was yet withheld from so doing, partly by a memory of my former crime, but chiefly by absolute **dread**.

My wife had called my attention, more than once, to the character of the white hair which constituted the sole visible difference between the strange beast and the one I had destroyed. By slow degrees—degrees nearly imperceptible, and which for a long time my Reason struggled to reject as fanciful—it had assumed a rigorous distinctness of outline.

It was now the representation of an object that I shudder to name— the Gallows! Neither by day nor by night knew I the blessing of Rest. During the former the creature left me no moment alone; and, in the latter, I started, hourly, from dreams of unutterable fear, to find the hot breath of **the thing** upon my face, and its vast weight—an **incarnate** Night-Mare that I had no power to shake off—incumbent eternally upon my **heart**!

How many mice were caught by the cat on the first day?

THE
BLACK CAT

THE
BLACK CAT

183

Solution on page 220

An Unmeasured Action

Beneath the pressure of such torments, the feeble remnant of the good within me succumbed, and the darkest and most evil thoughts became my sole intimates. From the sudden, ungovernable outbursts to which I now blindly abandoned myself, my uncomplaining wife was the most usual and patient of sufferers.

One day she accompanied me into the cellar of the old building which our poverty compelled us to inhabit. The cat followed me down the steep stairs, and, nearly throwing me headlong, exasperated me to madness. Uplifting an axe, and forgetting, in my wrath, the dread which had hitherto stayed my hand, I aimed a blow at the animal which would have proved instantly fatal had it descended as I wished. But this blow was arrested by the hand of my wife. Goaded, by the interference, into a rage more than demoniacal, I withdrew my arm from her grasp and buried the axe in her brain. She fell dead upon the spot, without a groan.

This hideous murder accomplished, I set myself forthwith to the task of concealing the body. I knew that I could not remove it without the risk of being observed. Many projects entered my mind. At one period I thought of cutting the corpse into minute fragments, and destroying them by fire. At another, I resolved to dig a grave in the floor of the cellar. I deliberated about casting it in the well in the yard, about packing it in a box, as if merchandise, and getting a porter to take it from the house. Finally I hit upon what I considered a far better expedient. I determined to wall it up in the cellar—as the monks of the middle ages are recorded to have walled up their victims. I made no doubt that I could readily displace the bricks, insert the corpse, and wall the whole up as before, so that no eye could detect anything suspicious.

The plan did not catch upon a single snare until I realised that the pails I had obtained for mixing the mortar were unsuitable—the formulation required five gallons of water and yet I only had a four-gallon pail and a seven-gallon pail, neither featuring any indications of measurement. A trifle! I soon deduced how to measure five gallons and set to work without delay.

THE
BLACK CAT

How could five gallons be measured?

Solution on page 220

The Fangs Of The Arch-Fiend

My next step was to look for the cause of so much wretchedness. Had I been able to find the **beast**, there could have been no doubt of its fate; but it appeared that the crafty animal had been alarmed and forebore to present itself in my present mood. It is impossible to describe the deep, blissful relief which its absence occasioned in my bosom. For one night at least, I soundly and tranquilly **slept**, even with the burden of murder upon my soul! The second and third day passed, and still my tormentor came not. The monster had fled forever! I should behold it no more! My happiness was supreme! The guilt of my deed disturbed me little. Upon the fourth day a party of the police arrived, unexpectedly, and proceeded to make rigorous investigation of the premises. Secure, however, in the inscrutability of my concealment, I felt no embarrassment. After a final search of the cellar, the officers were satisfied and prepared to depart. The glee in my heart was too strong to be restrained.

"Gentlemen," I said, "I delight to have allayed your suspicions. I wish you all health, and a little more courtesy. Here is a conundrum for you to take away on your travels! Take away one letter from me and I murder; take away two and I probably shall die, if my whole does not save me. By the bye, gentlemen, this—this is a very well constructed house. I may say an **excellently** well-constructed house. These walls—are you going, gentlemen?—these walls are solidly put together", and here, through the mere frenzy of **bravado** I rapped heavily upon that very portion of the brick-work behind which stood the corpse of my wife.

No sooner had the reverberation of my blows sunk into silence than I was answered by a voice from within the tomb!—by a cry, at first muffled and broken, then quickly swelling into one long, loud, continuous scream, utterly anomalous and inhuman—a howl—a wailing shriek, half of horror and half of triumph, such as might have arisen out of hell, conjointly from the throats of the damned in their agony and of the demons exulting in the damnation. For one instant the party remained motionless. In the next, a dozen stout arms were toiling at the wall. The corpse, already greatly decayed and clotted with gore, stood erect before the eyes of the spectators. Upon its head, with red extended mouth and solitary eye of fire, sat the hideous beast whose craft had seduced me into **murder**, and whose informing voice had consigned me to the hangman. I had walled the monster up within the tomb!

THE
BLACK CAT

186

"Take away one letter from me and I murder; take away two and I probably shall die, if my whole does not save me. What am I?"

THE
BLACK CAT

187

Solution on page 220

Edgar Allan Poe held the "faculty of resolution" in high esteem, hence his observation in one tale:

"As the strong man exults in his physical ability, delighting in such exercises as call his muscles into action, so glories the analyst in that moral activity which disentangles. He derives pleasure from even the most trivial occupations bringing his talents into play. He is fond of enigmas, of conundrums, of hieroglyphics; exhibiting in his solutions of each a degree of acumen which appears to the ordinary apprehension preternatural."

Imaginative puzzles consequently appear throughout the author's work, but never in such a high concentration as within his article *Enigmatical and Conundrum-ical* in the 18th December 1839 issue of *Alexander's Weekly Messenger*.

Why is a tin cup like a crab?

What must you do to a tea table to make it fit to consume?

Why is the Pacific like an inhabitant of Languedoc?

Why are murder and the English synonymous terms?

Why is a bleeding cat like a question?

Why are these conundrums like a song for one voice?

How many of Poe's conundrums can you solve?

ENIGMATICAL
AND CONUN-
DRUM-ICAL

ENIGMATICAL
AND CONUN-
DRUM-ICAL

189

Solution on page 221

Tales Of Ratiocination

Residing in Paris during the spring and part of the summer of 1840,
I there became acquainted with a Monsieur C. Auguste Dupin. This young
gentleman was of an illustrious family, but, by a variety of untoward
events, had been reduced to such poverty that the energy of his character
succumbed beneath it, and he ceased to bestir himself in the world or
care for the retrieval of his fortunes. Books, indeed, were his sole luxuries,
and in Paris these are easily obtained. Our first meeting was at an obscure
library in the Rue Montmartre, where the accident of our both being in
search of the same very rare and remarkable volume brought us into closer
communion. We saw each other again and again; above all, I felt my soul
enkindled by the wild fervour and the vivid freshness of his imagination.
I knew that the society of such a man would be a **treasure** beyond price,
and so it was arranged that we should live together.

Had the routine of life in our time-eaten and grotesque mansion been
known to the world, we should have been regarded as madmen. Our
seclusion was perfect. We admitted no visitors. We existed within ourselves
alone, busying ourselves in reading, writing, or conversing until
dark, then we sallied forth into the streets, arm and arm,
continuing the topics of the day, and seeking, amid
the wild lights and shadows of the city, that infinity
of mental excitement which observation can afford.
At such times I could not help remarking
and admiring a peculiar analytic ability
in Dupin. He seemed, too, to take delight in
its exercise, and did not hesitate to confess
the **pleasure** thus derived.

THE
MURDERS
IN THE RUE
MORGUE

He boasted to me, with a low chuckling laugh, that most men, in respect to himself, wore windows in their bosoms, and was wont to follow up such assertions by direct and startling proofs of his intimate knowledge of my own. Dupin told me of my youth, and how I was so close to my companions Isabel and Rose that even our sartorial choices were influenced by our proximity—how each day we would only wear red or white, but that whenever I wore red, Isabel would wear white, and how either Rose or myself would wear red but never both of us, and that Isabel and Rose would never wear white at the same time. He even knew what our possible clothing options were!

What were our possible clothing options?

Solution on page 221

Fathoming Cobblers

What I have described in the Frenchman was the result of an excited intelligence, but an example will best convey the character of his remarks. We were strolling one night down a long dirty street, in the vicinity of the Palais Royal. Being both, apparently, occupied with thought, neither of us had spoken for fifteen minutes at least.

All at once Dupin broke forth with these words: "She is a very little fellow, that's true, and would do better for the Théâtre des Variétés."

"There can be no doubt of that," I replied unwittingly, not at first observing the extraordinary manner in which the speaker had chimed in with my meditations. In an instant afterwards I recollected myself, and my astonishment was profound. "Dupin," said I, gravely, "this is beyond my comprehension. I can scarcely credit my senses. How do you know that I was thinking of—?" Here I paused, to ascertain beyond a doubt whether he really knew of whom I thought.

"—Rose," said he, "why do you pause? You were remarking to yourself that her diminutive figure unfitted her for tragedy." This was precisely what had formed the subject of my reflections. My childhood friend Rose was a former cobbler of the Rue St. Denis, who, becoming stage-mad, had attempted the role of Xerxes in Crébillon's tragedy and been notoriously lampooned for her pains. "Tell me, for Heaven's sake," I exclaimed, "the method by which you have been enabled to fathom my soul in this matter."

"I will explain," replied my friend, "and that you may comprehend all clearly, we will first retrace the course of your meditations." There was not a particle of charlatanry about Dupin.

"This month you ran into your former companions Isabel and Rose at the public baths. You had each begun attending last month. One of you attends the bath house every two days, another every three days, and the other every seven days. You went for the first time this month on a Monday, Isabel went for the first time this month on a Wednesday, and Rose went for the first time this month on a Friday. All I had to do to deduce what day of the month the unexpected meeting took place, then make ten or twelve other deductions which I am about to expound on at length, and *voila!*— I reasoned that you had been brought to the conclusion that the mender of soles was not of sufficient height for Xerxes. It was rather simple."

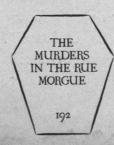

THE
MURDERS
IN THE RUE
MORGUE

192

What day of the month did the
unexpected meeting take place?

THE
MURDERS
IN THE RUE
MORGUE

193

Solution on page 221

Morning in the Rue Morgue

Not long after this, we were looking over an evening edition of the *Gazette des Tribunaux* when the following paragraphs arrested our attention:

"EXTRAORDINARY MURDERS.—The inhabitants of the Quartier St. Roch were aroused from sleep this morning by a succession of terrific shrieks issuing from the fourth story of a house in the Rue Morgue, known to be in the occupancy of one Madame L'Espanaye, her son Monsieur Pierre L'Espanaye, her daughter Madame Camille Mignaud and Madame M.'s son Monsieur Alexandre Mignaud. After some delay, the gateway was broken in with a crowbar, and eight neighbours entered, accompanied by two **gendarmes**. By this time the cries had ceased; but, as the party rushed up the stairs, three voices, in **angry** contention, were distinguished. **Isidor Musèt, gendarme,** deposes that he heard someone declare 'I am appalled. I wish I could be the mother of the victim, but I am not. It is the murderer who is my child!' **Henri Duval,** a neighbour, and by trade a silversmith, deposes that he also heard noises emanating from the floor, including, 'Well I am the mother of the victim and not the mother of the murderer!' **Pauline Dubourg,** laundress, confirms that she heard a voice say, 'I am the same sex as the **victim!**' but not why it was said.

"Upon arriving at the forth story, a spectacle presented itself which struck everyone present not less with horror than with astonishment. The apartment was in the wildest disorder—the furniture broken and thrown about in all directions. On a chair lay a razor, besmeared with blood. On the hearth were two or three long and thick tresses of grey human hair, also dabbled in blood, and seeming to have been pulled out by the roots. Of a body no traces were here seen; but an unusual quantity of soot being observed in the fireplace, a search was made in the chimney and a corpse was dragged therefrom; it having been thus forced up the narrow aperture for a considerable distance. The body was quite warm. Upon examining,

THE
MURDERS
IN THE RUE
MORGUE

Solution on page 222

the throat was so entirely cut that, upon an attempt to raise it, the head fell off. The body, as well as the head, was fearfully mutilated—the former so much so as scarcely to retain any semblance of humanity. It was evident to the attending officers that one of the four occupants of the home had been slain by one of the other three occupants, who had also been the ones to make the contentious statements. Additionally, the police maintained their conviction that one of the statements made by an occupant was a lie. To the horrible mystery posed by the question 'Who is the murderer?' there is not as yet, we believe, the slightest clue."

Dupin seemed singularly interested in the progress of this affair—at least so I judged from his manner. He asked me my opinion respecting the murders, and I could merely agree with all Paris in considering them an insoluble mystery. I saw no means by which it would be possible to trace the murderer; my friend believed otherwise.

"Who is the murderer?"

The Murders Down The Street

In the days that followed the arrest, as the city-wide fever inspired by the murder had finally broken, it became clear to me that something was playing on the mind of Dupin. Where once we would spend hours conversing, now he buried himself in books, daily papers and tomes on naturalism and comparative anatomy—to what end could not be gathered.

Of particular fascination to Dupin were other recent cases of barbarity and misrule. From the *Gazette des Tribunaux*, he read me a story concerning another murder in the the Quartier St. Roch—this one of a banker from the firm of Mignaud et Fils. Three men called William Bird, Adolphe Le Bon and Alberto Montani had all attended the banker's home on the night of the murder, and it was one of these men who was the guilty party.

The news report was patchy and oddly contrived—it mentioned, for instance, that the murderer had arrived at the house later than at least one of the other visitors, and that one of the police agents who would later investigate the crime arrived at midnight, and earlier than at least one of the other visitors. Additionally, neither Bird nor Le Bon arrived after midnight, the earlier arriver of Le Bon and Montani was not the police agent, and the later arriver of Bird and Montani was not the murderer.

"Who killed the banker, then?" I begged of Dupin, and after half an hour of outlining his elaborate reasoning he finally answered me.

THE
MURDERS
IN THE RUE
MORGUE

"Who killed the banker, then?"

THE
MURDERS
IN THE RUE
MORGUE

197

Solution on page 224

Deviations In Search For The True

The news that the alleged culprit had been falsely imprisoned was less astonishing than the revelation that even my esteemed friend César Auguste Dupin is not always right. For all of the logical precision of his deduction, there was a deeper, stranger explanation that would soon stretch one's belief to breaking point.

"Let us enter into some examinations for ourselves, before we make up an opinion respecting them," Dupin said. "An inquiry will afford us amusement."

I thought this an odd term, so applied, but said nothing. We proceeded at once to the Rue Morgue. The house was readily found; for there were still many persons gazing up at the closed shutters, with an objectless curiosity. Having shown our credentials, we were admitted by the agents in charge. We went upstairs—into the chamber where the body had been found, and where the deceased still lay. I saw nothing beyond what had been stated in the newspaper. Dupin scrutinized everything—not excepting the victim. The examination occupied us until dark, when we took our departure. He then asked me, suddenly, if I had observed anything peculiar at the scene of the atrocity. There was something in his manner of emphasizing the word which caused me to shudder, without knowing why.

"It appears to me that this mystery is considered insoluble, for the very reason which should cause it to be regarded as easy of solution," he noted.

"For instance, imagine I have given you a coin. You flip this coin 75 times and each time it comes up tails. If you flip it once more, which is most likely, heads or tails? Do you understand my point? The police are confounded by the seeming absence of motive—not for the murder itself. The wild disorder of the room; the corpse thrust up the chimney; the frightful mutilation of the body; these considerations have sufficed to paralyse the powers by putting completely at fault the boasted acumen of the government agents. They have fallen into the gross but common error of confounding the unusual with the abstruse. But it is by these deviations from the plane of the ordinary that reason feels its way in search for the true. It should not be asked 'what has occurred', so much as 'what has occurred that has never occurred before?'"

"Alright," I replied, accepting the lure, "what, then, has never occurred before?"

"I believe that nothing but an Orangutan could have committed this terrible deed!"

THE
MURDERS
IN THE RUE
MORGUE

198

Solution on page 224

If you flip it once more,
which is most likely,
heads or tails?

SOLUTIONS

CHAPTER 1: THE MASQUE OF THE RED DEATH

1 - A THIEF IN THE NIGHT
No, both knights were telling the truth. If the first knight had been lying then the statement would have been false and he couldn't have claimed incorrectly to be a liar. Accordingly his statement was true, meaning the second knight was also not lying, and neither had been exposed to the plague.

2 - LANDLOCKED LANDED GENTRY
If 810 of the guests had titles then 90 out of the 900 (100 had nothing) only had a fortune. As 630 of the guests had a fortune, that leaves 270 who only had a title. 270 + 90 = 360, which means 36% had one or the other but not both. Adding the 10% who had neither, that means 54% of the guests had both a fortune and a title, so 540 is the answer.

3 - A SPECTRE HAUNTS EUROPE
Yesterday.

4 - ANY COLOUR EXCEPT ONE
Venerio and Corelia were staying in the blue chamber; Maso and Galitia were in the green one; Antonio and Maria were staying in the purple apartment; while Girardino and Caterina were living in the orange apartment.

5 - A VOID
Scarlatto and Luzio didn't duel with each other.

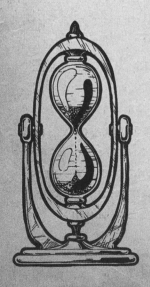

Solutions

6 – THE DANSE MACABRE

For simplicity, let's refer to the knights as A B C and D, and the dames as E F G and H. They must interact so that no-one dances either with or opposing another person twice.

	First room	Second room
1st dance	A G opposing B H	C E opposing D F
2nd dance	A H opposing C F	D E opposing B G
3rd dance	A F opposing D G	B E opposing C H

7 – THE APPLIANCES OF PLEASURE

Agnolo the improvisatore is first, followed by Amadore the harlequin, then Atenulf the ballet-dancer, then Andreuccio the buffoon, and finally Aiulf the musician.

8 – DARKNESS BURIES ALL

Nothing.

9 – THREE ELOQUENT WORDS

Poe wrote **A Valentine** for fellow poet Frances Sargent Osgood (although in his original version two years earlier he misspelled her middle name and called her a dunce). To find the answer, connect the first letter of the first line with the second letter of the second line, and so on:

For her this rhyme is penned, whose luminous eyes,

Brightly expressive as the twins of Lœda,

Shall find her own sweet name, that, nestling lies

Upon the page, enwrapped from every reader.

Search narrowly the lines!—they hold a treasure

Divine—a talisman—an amulet

That must be worn at heart. Search well the measure—

The words—the syllables! Do not forget

The trivialest point, or you may lose your labor!

And yet there is in this no Gordian knot

Which one might not undo without a sabre,

If one could merely comprehend the plot.

Enwritten upon the leaf where now are peering

Eyes scintillating soul, there lie perdus

Three eloquent words oft uttered in the hearing

Of poets, by poets—as the name is a poet's, too.

Its letters, although naturally lying

Like the knight Pinto—Mendez Ferdinando—

Still form a synonym for Truth.—Cease trying!

You will not read the riddle, though you do the best you *can* do.

Solutions

10 – THE CONQUEROR WORM

Spek is the only common word in the first two phrases, and likewise "trapped" is the only common word in the English version, so spek means "trapped". In the second and third foreign phrases, the word ruv is used, and the English translations share the word meaning "man", so, ruv means "man". We can see that the first and third phrases share the word maj, meaning "appearing". We can therefore deduce that in the first phrase "Maj hirmak spek", hirmak means "not". Likewise, the word twel from the second phrase means "help" and lursy from the third phrase must mean "dead". Therefore, to express "Help not dead"—assuming the language follows English syntax—you would say "Twel hirmak lursy".

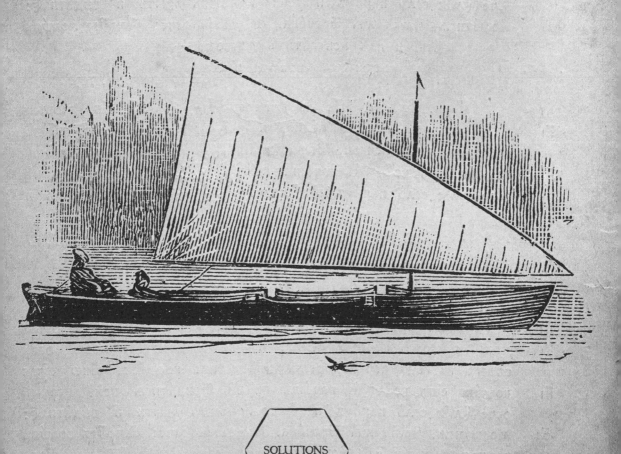

11 – FANCIES GROWN CHARNEL

.1 x .9 x .8 = .072 = 7.2%

12 – TORPID UNEASINESS

From the information given, we can calculate that there are 2100 throps in a pleem:

    1s = 10t
    1g = 6s = 6 x 10t = 60t
    1w = 5g = 5 x 60t = 300t
    1p = 7w = 7 x 300t = 2100t

We can also calculate that there are 30 slems in a wah:

    1w = 300t = 30(10t) = 30s

    2100 divided by 30 is 70.
    Therefore, the answer is 70.

13 – DEMONS ON THE OXUS

The two sons are both uncle and nephew to each other. To explain this, let's imagine the men are called Abner and Benjamin and their sons are Chauncy and Daniel. Benjamin and Chauncy are half-brothers because they have the same mother. Benjamin's son Daniel is therefore Chauncy's nephew. Likewise, Abner and Daniel are half-brothers, so Chauncy is Daniel's nephew. Benjamin's mother is married to Abner, so Benjamin's mother's stepmother is Abner's mother. This makes Abner's mother Benjamin's grandmother. Benjamin is therefore married to his grandmother, and is a grandfather to himself.

SOLUTIONS

206

Solutions

CHAPTER 2: THE RAVEN

14 – A VISITOR FROM ACHERON
The answer is a needle.

15 – A MURDER OF CROWS
The raven may have been giving the correct answer here: there would be no crows remaining in the tree as the others would fly away.

16 – OMINOUS RELATIONS OF YORE
TON. (Forward I am heavy, backwards I am not)

17 – BALM IN GILEAD
The raven is the bravest bird because it never wears the white feather.

18 – ALL THE JEWELS OF GOLCONDA AWAITING
The cipher is:

    a b c d e f g h i j k l m n o p q r s t u v w x y z
    5 2 — † 8 1 3 4 6 j k o 9 * ‡ . q ( ) ; ? ¶] x : z

Directly translated, the message reads:

    53‡‡†305))6*;4826)4‡.)4‡);806*;48†8¶60))85;;]8*;:‡*
    8†83(88)5*†;46(;88*96
    agoodglassinthebishopshostelinthedevilsseattwentyoned
    egreesandthirteenmi

?;8)‡(;485);5*†2:*‡(;4956*2(5*—4)8¶8*;4069285);)6†
8)4‡‡;1(‡9;48081;8:8‡

nutesnortheastandbynorthmainbranchseventhlimbeastsid
eshootfromthelefteyeo

1;48†85;4)485†528806*81(‡9;48;(88;4(‡?34;48)4‡;161;:
188;‡?;

fthedeathsheadabeelinefromthetreethroughtheshotfifty
feetout

Therefore the decoded message is:
> A good glass in the Bishop's hostel in the Devil's seat—twenty-one
> degrees and thirteen minutes—northeast and by north—main branch
> seventh limb east side—shoot from the left eye of the death's-head—
> a bee-line from the tree through the shot fifty feet out.

19 – THE PROPENSITY FOR PERVERSITY
One hour.

20 – A STEP OR TWO
200 feet.

21 – EXTINGUISHING A FLAME
The candles must have burned for three hours and 45 minutes (three
quarters) as one candle had one-sixteenth of its total length left and the
other had four-sixteenths.

22 – IF I BE NOT FOOL ENOUGH
Because it's a foul proceeding.

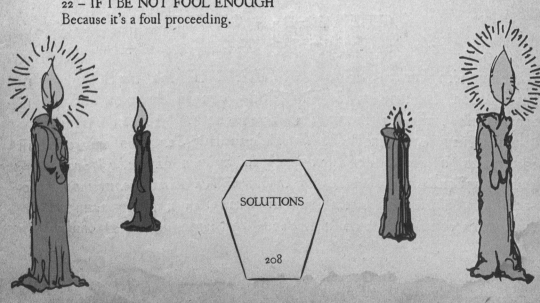

SOLUTIONS

CHAPTER 3: THE PIT AND THE PENDULUM

23 – DIFFERENT KINDS OF TORTURE

When the narrator drew the slip of paper, they could have immediately swallowed it. When the judges looked at the remaining slip they would have to agree that the narrator had drawn the PARDON.

24 – A JAR, AJAR

The narrator should put one red marble in one of the jars and the remaining 199 marbles in the other. This would have given them a 74.87% chance of being released. The probability of selecting either jar is 0.5, the probability of drawing a red marble from one jar is 1 and from the other jar is 99/199. Therefore, the overall probability is 0.5 x (1) + 0.5 x (99/199) = 0.7487.

25 – THE PUPPETS AND THE PARADE

The narrator and the other prisoners should have agreed that whoever was at the back of the line would say "black" if they saw an odd number of black hats and "red" if they saw an even number of black hats. While that prisoner couldn't improve or reduce their own chance of being set free, they could help the others.

     If the tenth prisoner says "black" and the ninth prisoner sees an odd number of black hats in front of him, they would know that their hat must be red, otherwise the tenth prisoner would have seen an even number of black hats. Equally, if the ninth prisoner sees an even number of black hats in front, they know that their own hat must be black, otherwise the tenth prisoner would have seen an even number of black hats. Each successive prisoner will need to deduce the colour of their own hat through logical reasoning.

     The first time a prisoner guesses "black" it signifies that an odd number of black hats is visible from the speaker's perspective. When the next prisoner says "black", it must signify that an even number of black hats is visible from the speaker's perspective. Each time someone says "black", the signification changes. Knowing this, each prisoner is able to deduce the colour of their own hat based on the number of times they hear the

prisoners behind them say "black", and the number of black hats they can see in front of themself. This plan guarantees that nine of the prisoners will be set free, with the one at the back having a 50/50 chance.

26 – THE BEAST LIES IN WAIT
The beast is behind the fourth door.

27 – A DARK AND FINAL ABYSS
A chain.

28 – LIFE'S UNANTICIPATED PITFALLS
The third door could be immediately ruled out, as if it was safe then both of its statements would be false. As the first statements on the first and second doors agree, they are either both true or false. If they were false then their second statements would be true, which isn't possible as those statements contradict each other. This means their first statements are true and the second door is the safe one.

29 – THE GATHERING SQUALL
Four and a half hours.

30 – UP IN FLAMES
The rope is 32 ft. 1 1/2 inches in length from the floor to the ceiling, so the narrator will be able to escape.

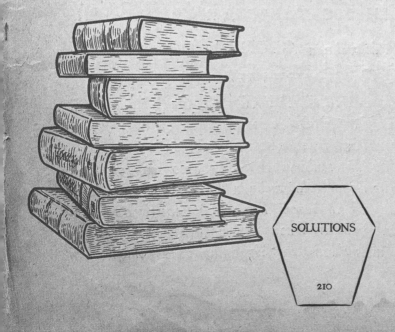

SOLUTIONS

Solutions

31 – BRILLIANT BUT UNLICENSED
Line - author:

1 – Spenser
2 – Homer
3-4 – Aristotle
5-6 – Kallimachos
7 8 Shelley
9 – Alexander Pope
10 – Euripides
11 – Mark Akenside
12 – Samuel Rogers
13-14 – Euripides
15-16 – William Shakespeare

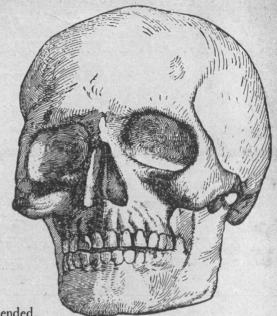

32 – A HORRIBLE IMPROBABILITY
The former are dead men, the latter are mended.

33 – ODD TRAINS OF THOUGHT
The two engines will be the same distance from Rockwood when they meet.

34 – STILLING THE RATTLE
The important point here is that the man in yellow is talking to Mr. White and so cannot be him. Nor can he be Mr. Yellow, since nobody is wearing his own colour. So the man in yellow must be Mr. Black. Mr. White cannot be wearing white, so he's in black. That leaves Mr. Yellow wearing white.

35 – THINGS TO COME
The only relationship these letters have is that their uppercase shapes are totally or partially closed. R is the next and final letter of the alphabet that meets this requirement.

36 – THE LIVING END
Fire.

SOLUTIONS

Solutions

CHAPTER 4: THE CASK OF AMONTILLADO

37 – MISTAKEN MAY MERRYMAKING
The earliest date for the Mardi Gras of the story would be 8th May and the latest would be 14th May.

38 – PIPE PRICING POINT
The narrator originally had 96 Lira.

39 – CATACOMB COLLECTION COUNTING
Nine bottles of wine.

40 – BOTTLE-BARTERING BUTLER
The wine originally cost 798 Lira so to gain 5% the merchant must receive 837.90. He now charges the narrator 931 Lira, so that when the merchant and the butler each receive their 5% cut the merchant will get 737.90.

41 – SPLITTING STOLEN SUPPLIES
There were 24 bottles in total and the equivalent of 21 full bottles of wine to be divided, and as three is the only number which divides into both quantities, there must have been three robbers. One robber could have taken 3 full demi-bottles, 1 empty demi-bottle, 1 full standard-bottle and 3 empty standard-bottles. Each of the others would then take 2 full demi-bottles and 2 empty ones, along with 3 full standard-bottles and 1 empty one, so each man would get three and a half standard-bottle's worth of wine, and 4 empty standard and 4 empty demi-bottles.

42 – FORTUNATO'S FAMILY FRUSTRATION
Onesta is Tortula's niece.

SOLUTIONS

Solutions

43 – CALLOW CRYPT CONUNDRUMS
Death.

44 - A FLIGHT IN THE AERIAL
Mr Henson wasn't alone in his journey. When the hot air balloon ran into difficulty, he and his companions shed their clothes but were still carrying too much weight. They drew toothpicks to see who would sacrifice themselves and Mr Henson lost. After jumping to his death, his companions flew to safety and concealed their identities.

45 – RULED BY A SPITEFUL CHILD
Lanval must be Carbuncle, Gille must be Toad, Aucassin has to be Disappointed-his-parents, and Flore must be Turkey brain.

46 – THE GHOSTS OF WIT
Actually, the yolk is yellow.

47 – A CRUEL PLAYTHING
A hole.

48 – SETTING A LURE
The masquerade started at 19:00.

49 – THE SWINE
P G (pig without an I).

50 – BAL DES ARDENTS
If Hop Frog had used both torches he could have killed the men in 1.2 minutes, or 72 seconds.

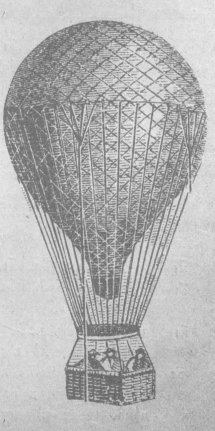

SOLUTIONS

CHAPTER 5: THE FALL OF THE HOUSE OF USHER

51 – BESIDE A BLACK AND LURID TARN
Because they both contain many currants/currents.

52 – FLOWN OFF THE THREAD
The conclusion is false. Some shrabs may be losas, but it is not definite.

53 – AN ATMOSPHERE PECULIAR
Roosters don't lay eggs.

54 – THE DIMENSIONS OF MADNESS
Suppose x is the diagonal of the floor, then $x, = 24, + 48,, x = 24 \sqrt{5}$
If h is the height of the room, then $h, + (24 \sqrt{5}), = 56$, and $h = 16$,
therefore, the height of the room is 16ft.

55 – A STRUGGLE WITH THE GRIM PHANTASM
Yes. Assume that there is 200,000 people in the town. If each inhabitant had a different number of hairs on their head then there would be 200,000 different positive whole numbers each less than 200,000, which is impossible.

56 – TORN OR FRAYING HEARTS
You would say queg ool (note that the adjectives follow the nouns).
The words are:

    holver = fraying
    plu = mend
    queg = heart
    jire = robes
    ool = torn
    kleest = often

SOLUTIONS

57 – THE TERRORS HE HAD ANTICIPATED
The letter F is like death because it makes all fall.

58 – NAMES THAT LIE CONCEALED
The poem was written for Poe's acquaintance Sarah Anna Lewis. To spell out her name, add the first letter of the first line, the second letter of the second line, and so on.

> "Seldom we find," says Solomon Don Dunce,
> "Half an idea in the profoundest sonnet.
> Through all the flimsy things we see at once
> As easily as through a Naples bonnet—
> Trash of all trash!—how can a lady don it?
> Yet heavier far than your Petrarchan stuff—
> Owl-downy nonsense that the faintest puff
> Twirls into trunk-paper the while you con it."
> And, veritably, Sol is right enough.
> The general tuckermanities are arrant
> Bubbles—ephemeral and so transparent—
> But this is, now,—you may depend upon it—
> Stable, opaque, immortal—all by dint
> Of the dear names that lie concealed within 't.

59 – HABITS OF RIGID THOUGHT
56 of the crew have worked for both the Dutch East India Company and the John Company. As 13 crewmembers have never sailed before, we're left with 87 who have some sailing experience. Of those 87 crewmembers, 78 have worked for the John Company, which means that 9 have not (87 - 78 = 9). 65 crewmembers have worked for the Dutch East India Company, meaning that 22 haven't (87 - 65 = 22). Therefore, there are 9 + 22 or 31 people who could not have had experience working for both companies, and 87 - 31 or 56 people who have.

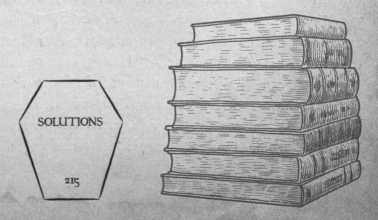

SOLUTIONS

60 – UNDER THE WEATHER

If the quantity of cotton-wool is doubled every minute, and the sack is completely filled after two hours, then the sack would be half-filled a minute before that. Therefore, the narrator was below deck for an hour and 59 minutes.

61 – A STRIPPED DECK

11 rounds of cards were played. The Swede had to win four rounds to draw even with the narrator, and then the Swede had to win three more times: $4 + 4 + 3 = 11$.

62 – CALM SEAS, PROSPEROUS VOYAGE

The sons had decided to switch boats – the son whose skiff arrived last would inherit the estate, so if they used each other's vessels then they would each try to finish first.

63 – SOME WATERY HELL

When she lies at the wharf.

64 – LIKE GHOSTS OF BURIED CENTURIES

"Congra" means Simoom. From the first two phrases, "glup" must mean approaching. From the third phrase, "terook" must mean immense, leaving "congra" to be Simoom.

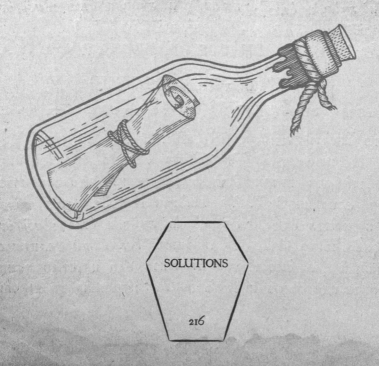

CHAPTER 6: THE TELL-TALE HEART

65 – COLD DISCOVERY
Unquestionably.

66 – BURNS AND BURNS
A lantern.

67 – SLEEPING DOGS
The old man had four dogs: a Plott Hound, a Blue Lacy, a Mountain Feist and a Cur.

68 – KILLING TIME
It will take 12.83 seconds for the clock to strike 12. At 7 o'clock, there were 6 intervals between the 7 gongs, and as it took 7 seconds from first to last gong, that means each gong interval is 7/6 seconds. At midnight there will be 11 intervals, therefore it will take (11 x 7/6) seconds, or 12.83 seconds.

69 – THE BEGINNING OF THE END
The letter E.

70 – THE BURYING OF HIS HIDEOUS HEART!
To arrive at the answer, the task needs to be divided among the two characters so they finish at the same time. The narrator can dispose of a body 1½ times faster than the old man so they should do 1½ times the work: the old man should do 2/5 of the disposing and the narrator should do 3/5 of it. As the narrator dismembered and concealed the corpse in two hours they could do 3/5 of the job in 1 and 1/5 hours (3/5 x 2). This means the fastest time they could dispose of the old man working together (putting aside the issue of him being dead and in bits) is 1 hour and 12 minutes. As the narrator finished at 04:00, he must have started at 02:00, so if the pair had done the task together they would have finished at 03:12.

71 – A LOW, DULL, QUICK SOUND

1000 kilometres. A cubic metre equals 1000 cubic millimetres x 1000 x 1000. One thousand millimetre cubes placed on top of each other would make a 1 metre tall pole, and as there is 1000 x 1000 times more cubes, there would be a pole that is 1000 kilometres in height.

72 – POEM FOR A HERRING

Elizabeth Rebecca (Herring).

73 – A PRESSBURG EDUCATION

Yes, it is possible. There are 365 days in a non-leap year and 52 weeks in a year, and 52 x 7 = 364, meaning there is one extra day. Therefore the probability of any one day of the week occurring in a non-leap year is one-seventh.

74 – LIKE A SHADOW UPON THE SOUL

Morella will reach the destination first. To prove this, let's suppose they cover 12 miles, both walking at a speed of 2 miles per hour and running at a speed of 6 miles per hour.

rt = d (rate X time = distance) to find each person's time.

The narrator, walking half the distance and running half the distance:
2t = 6 miles, so t = 3 hours walking
6t = 6 miles, so t = 1 hour running
t = 4 hours total time

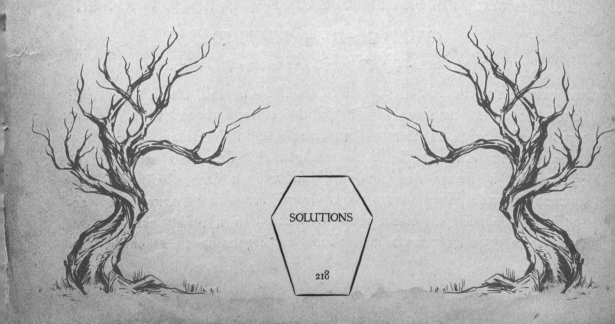

SOLUTIONS

Morella, walking half the time and running half the time.

$2(1/2t) + 6(1/2t) = 12$ miles

$t + 3t = 12$

$4t = 12$

$t = 3$ hours total time

75 – PRINCIPIUM INDIVIDUATIONIS
The letter Q.

76 – MORELLA!
The answer is 50. 48 is the midpoint between 28 and 68, so we need to find the midpoint between 24 and 76. Adding together 24 and 76 makes 100, and dividing that by 2 makes 50.

CHAPTER 7: THE BLACK CAT

77 – EARLY BEASTS AND BIRDS
There are 30 beasts and 15 birds. Let's use b to represent the number of beasts and B to represent the number of birds. From the total number of feet it's possible to deduce that:

B(2 feet/bird) + b(4 feet/beast) = 150, or

$2B + 4b = 150$

The total number of animals is $B + b = 45$

so $B = 45 - b$

This last equation can be used in the feet equation:

$2(45 - b) + 4b = 150$

$90 - 2b + 4b = 150$

$2b = 60$

$b = 30$ beasts and $B = 45 - 30 = 15$ birds

Solutions

78 – A BOTTLE UNCORKED
The letter N.

79 – WRONG FOR WRONG'S SAKE
The narrator's previous drink was gin.

80 – HOMEWARD BOUND
The house number is 204 and there are 288 houses on the narrator's side of the street—none of the other solutions (such as if the house number was 6 with 8 houses on the street, or if the house number was 1189 with 1681 houses in all) are valid as there must be between 50 and 500 houses.

81 – MARKED FOR THE SCAFFOLD
The cat killed no mice on the first day. It killed 3, 6, 9, and 12 mice on the second, third, fourth, and fifth days, respectively. If m represents the number of mice caught on the first day:

$$m + (m + 3) + (m + 6) + (m + 9) + (m + 12) = 30$$
$$m + m + 3 + m + 6 + m + 9 + m + 12 = 30$$
$$5m + 30 = 30$$
$$5m = 0$$
$$m = 0$$

82 – AN UNMEASURED ACTION
To measure five gallons with a four-gallon and seven-gallon pail, the narrator can start by filling the four-gallon pail with water and pouring it into the empty seven-gallon paid. Then, they should fill the four-gallon paid again and pour as much as they can into the seven-gallon pail until it is full. This will leave a single gallon in the four-gallon bucket. After emptying the seven-gallon pail and transferring the single gallon, the narrator can then fill the four-gallon pail again and pour it into the seven-gallon pail, producing exactly five gallons.

83 – THE FANGS OF THE ARCH-FIEND
Skill (take away one for kill, two for ill).

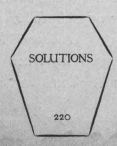

SOLUTIONS

84 – SONGS FOR ONE VOICE

Why is a tin cup like a crab? Because it is a can, sir (a cancer).

What must you do to a tea table to make it fit to consume? Take tea (t) from it, then it becomes eatable.

Why is the Pacific like an inhabitant of Languedoc? Because it's a languid ocean (a Languedocian).

Why are murder and the English synonymous terms? Because the English are assassination. (A sassy nation).

Why is a bleeding cat like a question? Because it's a catty gory (category).

Why are these conundrums like a song for one voice? Because they're so low (solo).

85 – TALES OF RATIOCINATION

There are only two feasible options for the friends: for the narrator to wear white and for Isabel and Rose to wear red, or for the narrator and Isabel to wear white and for Rose to wear red.

86 – FATHOMING COBBLERS

Dupin makes three statements:

(1) The narrator, Isabel and Rose each began attending the public baths last month.

(2) One attends every two days, another every three days and the other every seven days.

(3) The narrator attended for the first time this month on a Monday, Isabel for the first time this month on a Wednesday, and Rose for the first time this month on a Friday.

It can be deduced from (1) and (2) that the two-day person went to the baths for the first time that month on the 1st or the 2nd and the three-day person went for the first time that month on the 1st, 2nd, or 3rd. As there are two days between each person's first attendance that month, from (3) it can be deduced that the two-day person went on the 1st and the three-day person went on the 3rd. Considering all three statements it can be deduced that the seven-day person went for the first time that month on either the 5th or 6th.

This means that one of two options are true:

a. The narrator went on Monday, the 1st and every two days after that, Isabel went on Wednesday, the 3rd and every three days after that, and Rose went on Friday, the 5th and every seven days after that. If this is the case then their attendance dates would be as follows:

The narrator: 1, 3, 5, 7, 9, 11, 13, 15, 17, 19, 21, 23, 25, 27, 29, 31

Isabel: 3, 6, 9, 12, 15, 18, 21, 24, 27, 30

Rose: 5, 12, 19, 26

b. Isabel went on Wednesday, the 1st and every two days after that, Rose went on Friday, the 3rd and every three days after that, and the narrator went on Monday, the 6th and every seven days after that. If this is the case then their attendance dates would be:

Isabel: 1, 3, 5, 7, 9, 11, 13, 15, 17, 19, 21, 23, 25, 27, 29, 31

Rose: 3, 6, 9, 12, 15, 18, 21, 24, 27, 30

The narrator: 6, 13, 20, 27

As the three friends attended the bath on the same day that month, the first option cannot be accurate. This means the second one is correct, and therefore the narrator, Isabel and Rose met on Monday, the 27th.

87 – MORNING IN THE RUE MORGUE

Madame L'Espanaye committed the murder. Three statements were made:

A. I am the mother of the murderer, but not mother of the victim
B. I am the mother of the victim but not the mother of the murderer.
C. I am the same sex as the victim

If the first two statements are true then a different woman would have made each one and a man would have made the third statement. The first two statements would mean that the victim was a man, which would contradict the third statement being false. This would mean that either A or B is false and C is true.

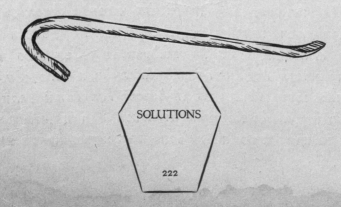

Solutions

If C was a true statement by a woman then A and C would each be made by a different man, which means both statements would be false and would contradict C, which would be impossible. That would mean that C was a true statement made by a man, which would make the victim a man, and one of the statements A or B would be made by Madame Camille and the other by her mother, with either Camille's brother or son as the victim.

If statement B is false then there are different outcomes to consider. If Camille's brother was the victim, Camille's mother could not have made true statement A, so her mother made false statement B and Camille is the murderer. That would mean however that Camille would have had to made true statement A, which is impossible. Alternately, if Camille's son is the victim, Camille could not have made true statement A, so she made false statement B and her son is also the murderer. This is also impossible. Therefore, statement B isn't false.

This means that statement A is the false statement, which also presents different outcomes. If Camille's brother is the victim, her mother made true statement B, Camille isn't the murderer and made false statement A, which means Camille's son isn't the murderer and Camille's mother is the murderer. Alternately, if Camille's son is the victim, Alice made true statement B, her mother made false statement A, neither Camille nor her brother are the murderer, and Camille's mother is the culprit. In either case, Camille's mother Madame L'Espanaye is the murderer, but it is not possible to tell who the victim was or who made each statement.

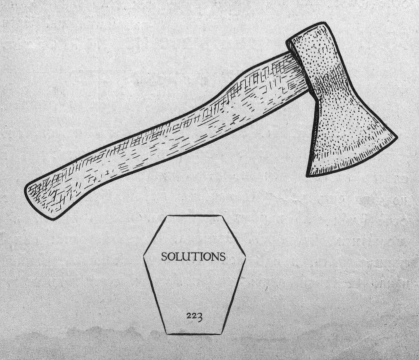

SOLUTIONS

88 – THE MURDERS DOWN THE STREET

William Bird. It can be deduced that the police agent arrived at midnight and at least one of the other visitors arrived after midnight. We see that Alberto Montani arrived after midnight, meaning he wasn't the police agent. We can also observe that Adolphe Le Bon was not the police agent, which means that William Bird must have been. Therefore it follows that Alberto Montani is innocent and William Bird arrived after Adolphe Le Bon, and this means that William Bird was both the police agent and the murderer.

89 – DEVIATIONS IN SEARCH FOR THE TRUE

Tails is the most likely answer. If a coin shows tails each time on 75 flips, and we're provided with no evidence that it is regular coin, then it is surely a coin with tails on both sides. As Dupin says: "It is by these deviations from the plane of the ordinary that reason feels its way in search for the true."